ONE HOP TOO FAR

ONE HOP TOO FAR

I Opened my Heart to Ethiopia

Jane Graham

The Book Guild Ltd
Sussex, England

The Book Guild Ltd
25 High Street,
Lewes, Sussex

First published 1999
© Jane Graham, 1999

Set in Times by
Rowland Phototypesetting Ltd
Bury St Edmunds, Suffolk

Printed in Great Britain by
Bookcraft (Bath) Ltd, Avon

A catalogue record for this book is
available from the British Library

ISBN 1 85776 368 8

CONTENTS

Encompassed on all sides by the enemies of their religion, the Aethiopians slept near a thousand years, forgetful of the world, by whom they were forgotten.

Edward Gibbon, *The History of the Decline and Fall of the Roman Empire*

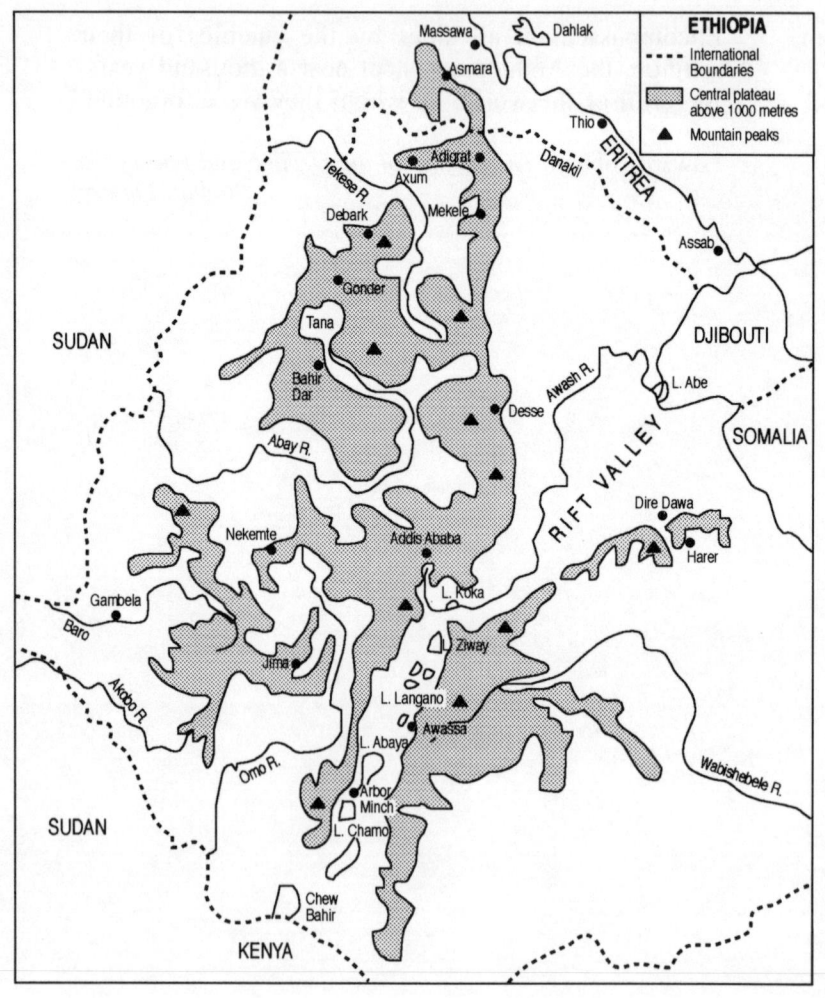

INTRODUCTION

I did not set out to write another guide book to Ethiopia. There are already several very good ones that provide all the detailed information a traveller needs. Rather I wanted to convey some idea of how much fun can be had travelling in this extraordinary country, how much variety there is of landscape and people, and to outline some of the journeys that I made that might give other prospective travellers some ideas about where to go. If you are like me and have the urge to explore the various nooks and crannies of a country, you are bound to encounter the frustrations I did. The rough roads, intractable officials and Spartan accommodation will get you down from time to time. But in Ethiopia these hazards are more than offset by the universal friendliness of the common people, the readiness to welcome you and the ease with which, even where there's no common language, one can fit in with what's going on around. These are the qualities one remembers and the reason why travel in Ethiopia really can be so enjoyable.

Ethiopia is a fascinating country to travel around for many reasons. The astonishing variety of people – some 80 or so languages are in daily use around the country, each one reflecting a unique people with a distinctive culture – is one. The many vestiges of former civilisations – castles, curious churches, huge monoliths, fields of stelae of uncertain origin – is another. Beyond historical times rock paintings of Stone Age cultures and before them the relics of the very ancestors of the human race provide yet more intriguing things to see. All this is absorbing enough by itself but set as it is in a stupendous range of landscapes from searing deserts below sea level to cold, high mountains makes it all the more remarkable.

1

To fully appreciate the role Ethiopia has played in the history of Christianity and of north-eastern Africa one needs to look first at its distinctive geography. The dominant physical feature of Ethiopia is the high central plateau that has played such a significant role in the country's history. The Ethiopian highlands that comprise the greater part of the country were formed 40 million years ago by a vast outpouring of lava. These basalts have weathered into fertile soils that, combined with the high rainfall of high ground, have allowed very large numbers of people to make a relatively easy living off the land. Thus Ethiopia, with only 4 per cent of Africa's land, supports 8 per cent of the continent's population.

But before modern man made his appearance, the great central highland massif was split in two by another spectacular geological event – The Great Rift Valley. This was first formed (in fact it is still forming) about 13 million years ago when continental plates pulled apart and the earth's crust subsided in between. The faulting instigated extensive volcanic eruptions in and alongside the rift valley creating numerous high mountains, hot springs and many still-active volcanoes. Along the valley floor many lakes were formed by the rivers draining the fringing highlands. The abundant water of these lakes created a lush environment that some 9 million years later became the legendary Garden of Eden – the place where man emerged.

As well as creating a wet, fertile environment highly suited to humans the great highland massif also set the stage for the evolution of the many endemic species of plants and animals for which Ethiopia is famous. Its immense size and isolation from other highland massifs were the main reasons for this. Half of all Africa's highlands above 2000 metres are in Ethiopia and over 80 per cent of all land over 3000 metres. This made, in effect, a huge island of high ground in which all sorts of unique plants and animals – many still undescribed – evolved as a result of their isolation.

Ethiopia borders on Eritrea to the north, Sudan to the west, Djibouti and Somalia to the east, and Kenya to the south. Culturally, it is one of the oldest nations in the world with a recorded history going back 3000 years. The legendary land of Punt along the Red Sea coast of what is nowadays Eritrea, Djibouti and Somalia was known in 2500 BC. The legendary Queen of Sheba (ruler of Saba, the ancient kingdom that straddled the Red Sea) visited King Solomon in Jerusalem around 1000 BC and their child was Menelik I, the first in a long line of Ethiopian kings. Menelik II, 3000 years later in 1889 founded Addis Ababa, today's capital of Ethiopia.

Five main roads leave Addis Ababa. The road to the north-west leads to Bahir Dar on Lake Tana, then to Gondar and on to Axum. It also serves the remote areas of north-west Ethiopia along the Sudan border. Directly to the north through Dese and Mekele goes the highway to Asmara, the Eritrean capital that lies inland from the port of Massawa on the Red Sea. Leaving the city to the east is the highway to Assab, the other Eritrean port on the Red Sea. This road branches at Mojo, 100 kilometres out of Addis. The branch to Assab takes a north-easterly direction, while the branch to the south serves Awassa and many other centres before continuing on to Kenya. The branch to the east serves Dire Dawa and Harar on its way to the Djibouti coast. A fourth highway – the Jima road – winds south-west through lush green coffee country to the tropical rainforests of the Illuababor highlands, before descending into the steamy, swampy country on the south-western Ethiopian border. Lastly there is the western highway that serves Nekemte and other centres of western Ethiopia.

I should like to say that I probably never would have made these journeys without the company, advice and assistance of my friend Cherent Zewide. Cherent spent all his annual leave for the past three years travelling with me. Driving with someone who speaks Amharic (not to mention Orominia and English and Tigrinya) smoothes out innumerable potential hassles, but that was the least of his contribution. He got us back on the right track when we missed the way, fixed breakdowns, ensured that I paid the right price for things and protected me from the worst of marauding children and beggars. But more than anything his patient, easy manner and sense of humour made it easy for me to sit down with strangers from everywhere in Ethiopia and have a chat and a drink and a laugh with them. And that's what really turns travel into fun.

3

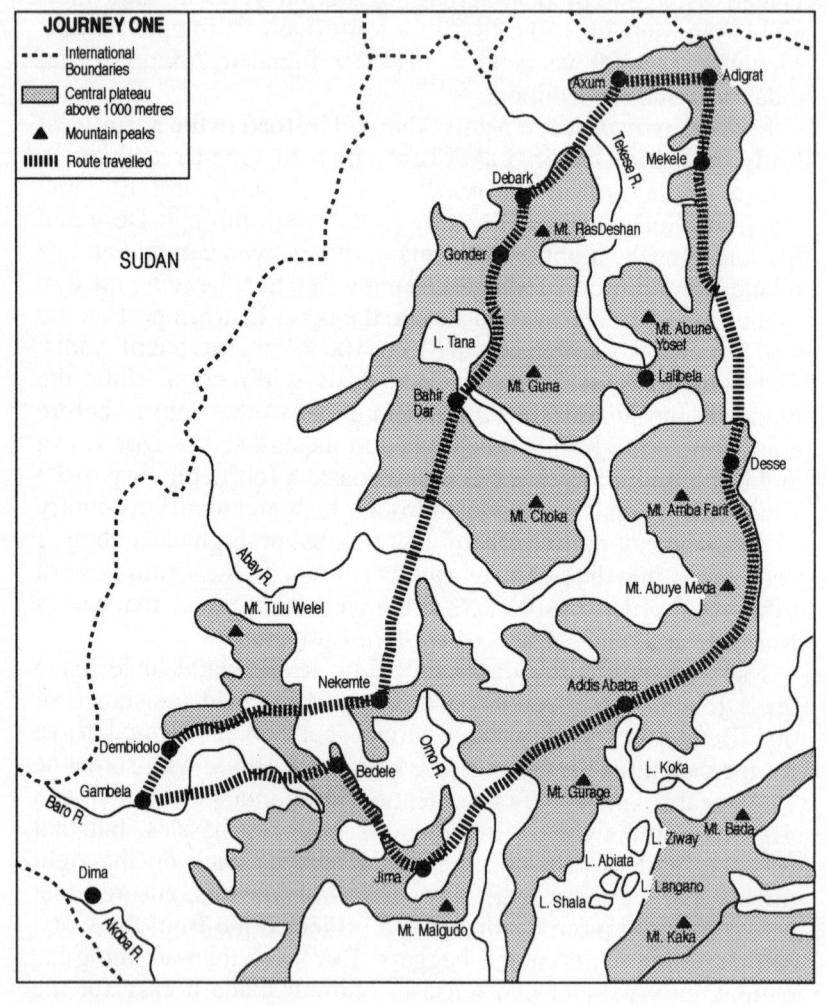

1

Everywhere

Since coming to Ethiopia in mid-1995 I had been working hard to finish a series of paintings. The moment the work was done and an exhibition date marked on my Ethopian Airlines calendar I knew that it was time to get out of town and look for adventure in this amazing country. I had already been here for four months, or, should I say, I had been confined to my studio for four months, never venturing more than a few kilometres away to shop, or to visit the office. So I went to the office and found my friend, Cherent, sitting there twiddling his thumbs. I reminded him of what he had promised me a few months earlier. 'Janey,' he'd said, 'I will take you wherever you want to go. Just let me know.' Here in Ethiopia I am known as Janey because in Amharic an 'e' at the end of a word tends to be pronounced. His promise still held and fortunately he had two weeks leave due which his department was trying to force him to take because the end of the financial year was just around the corner. Leave cannot be carried forward and days not taken during the year in question are forfeit.

Within a few hours of my office visit we'd put a deposit down on a hired Pajero four-wheel drive and we were on our way to the nearest fuel station to fill up for the journey. All this happened in such quick succession that I hadn't even thought about where we were going to travel. At the fuel station Cherent turned to me and said, 'Well, where are we going?' I replied, 'Everywhere.' But going everywhere at once is not feasible, and so we had to choose a direction. We chose the south-west.

The next morning we left for 'everywhere' in the direction of Gambela, to the south-west of Addis Ababa. Gambela is on the border with Sudan, low-lying flat land beyond the edge of the Ethiopian highlands. The town is on the Baro river, one of the many rivers draining the south-west Ethiopian highlands. I must admit I was a little apprehensive on departure, knowing hardly anything about either Ethiopia or Cherent.

From the tourist map I saw that there were plenty of towns and villages on our route, so it was not going to be like driving across a desert or doing a ten-day foot safari as far as having to think carefully about what we had to take with us. Food, water, accommodation and fuel were going to be available all along the route so all I needed to pack were a few clothes and of course a jack, wheel brace, spare tyres and a few tools.

As I was doing this, I remembered a two-week walking trip I once did in 1990 in the very north of the Central African Republic with three porters and an old Muslim elephant hunter. I was out to take photographs of elephants and I had carefully planned every detail of that walk in order not to worry every night about the following day. Nevertheless, at the beginning of the trip when I was dropped off some 100 kilometres from the main camp, and watched the Land Rover speed away, my heart seemed to drop to my stomach. I wanted to sit down and cry, rather than start pushing my way through the tangled forest on the river bank. Well, I have had many adventures in different parts of Africa and I have always been lucky to come out on top. This trip ought not to prove more of a challenge than any of the others, and I didn't have any misgivings as we drove out of Addis.

All being well our first night would be spent in Jima, some 375 kilometres south-west of Addis. The scenery during the journey changed dramatically as we went along. About 55 kilometres from Addis Ababa between Tefki and Teji we passed through flat black-cotton country covered in crops. This area is part of the Awash River floodplain, fertile land supporting large numbers of farmers. The Awash is a quiet stream in the dry season but in the wet season it swells into a vast, brown torrent that frequently overflows its banks and submerges large areas of the surrounding farmlands. On a later journey to Jima, in this same area, I saw

6

the farmers converging on the villages to load fertiliser on their donkeys to take to their farms. On the way back from Jima two weeks later, all the fields were under water. The farmers were out fortifying the dikes to protect their homes from the flood. The fertiliser was now in the river on its way to Asaita near the Red Sea where the Awash River finally disappears in the Danakil desert. But on this first trip I didn't know about the turmoil that the flooding Awash could cause. The sun was shining on the green fields, lighting up the *tef* swaying in the gentle breeze, and my heart opened to Ethiopia.

About 100 kilometres from Addis we passed through Welisso, a small town with an attractive hotel, the Welisso Hotel, one of the state-owned Ethiopia Hotel chain, built in what used to be a forest with a hot spring. There were two large spring-fed swimming pools at the place, one outside surrounded by bougainvillaea, and another very large one inside, near the bedrooms. The former emperor Haile Selassie used to patronise this hotel with his family, and the building had clearly been very luxurious in former times. Nowadays, though, it is run-down and badly in need of repair. Haile Selassie, born Tafari Makonnen, was the son of Ras Makonnen, and spent much of his early childhood in Harar, in eastern Ethiopia, where his father was the first governor. In 1930 Ras Tafari assumed the imperial throne of Ethiopia as the Emperor Haile Selassie, King of Kings, Lion of Judah. He was the last of a long line of kings going back in legend to King Solomon and the Queen of Sheba. In 1974 the imperial government was overthrown by the Dergue revolution that introduced a hard-line socialist government. The aged Haile Selassie was suffocated as he slept and Ethiopian hereditary monarchies ended forever.

Between Welisso and the next small town, Welkite, there was an abundance of a certain style of hut, circular with a very evenly thatched and extremely tall conical roof. These I was told were Gurage houses. The area between the two small towns was extensively farmed by the Gurage people who have lived there for a few hundred years. The Gurage are a skilful people with a gift for organisation. They are also a very adaptable people who are ready to accept any form of modernisation. They believe that

7

idleness is a sin and failure to improve one's land is purely bad farming. The key to success is work. They are not only successful farmers but also rich traders. Here outside Welisso the rolling green country was heavily dotted with meticulously kept little farms. Little groups of houses were frequently surrounded by a wild banana plant called *enset*, the tubers of which are ground into a flour from which a rather stodgy, grey bread called *kocho* is made, the Gurage staple. For many Gurage, their entire lives revolve round the annual cycle of the *enset*.

At first the road out of Welkite passed through more green cultivated land interspersed with forest before beginning to descend into the Omo valley. Here there was an exciting stretch of road, with rocky outcrops and thick acacia forest on the hills, a great contrast to the flat land of the farms. 188 kilometres from Addis Ababa, and 44 kilometres from Welkite, we came across the large bridge over the Gibe River, which, at that point changes its name to the Omo. Near the bridge we saw some shanty tea and pasty stalls where we stopped and had a welcome cup of thick sweet tea. Cherent told me that it was at this point on the river that tourists can start a 21-day river run down the spectacular Omo River gorge. There is plenty of white water when the river is low and the more inaccessible parts give refuge to one of the last surviving populations of hippo in Ethiopia, still some several hundred strong. The trip ends at the ferry crossing into Omo National Park.

We arrived in Jima just before dark. On the drive to the town the vegetation gradually grew much thicker, eventually becoming dense forest. Much of the forest was wild coffee shaded by acacia and cedar trees. The town itself was lush and green. Jima is the largest town in south-west Ethiopia and the capital of Jima Zone in Oromia Region, one of Ethiopia's major coffee growing areas. The coffee bush *Coffea arabica* evolved in the highland forests of Ethiopia, particularly those of the south-west, and today these forests harbour the world's most important remaining reservoir of wild varieties of the bush. In fact, Ethiopians, who are keen coffee drinkers, were probably the first people to make a tradition of the habit. Gradually, cultivation of the coffee bush spread to southern Arabia via the south-east Ethiopian highlands around

Harar and from Arabia the use of coffee spread to other parts of the world.

Jima also lies not so far from Masha, the wettest place in Ethiopia, where more than 2500 mm of rain falls annually. In earlier times, great trade routes used to pass through this town because of the ease of travel, as there were no huge mountains to climb or deep rivers and gorges to cross. In the sixteenth century the Oromo people moved across the south of Ethiopia conquering and absorbing the Kingdom of Jima, and it still belongs to them. Jima kings used to live in palaces, surrounded by soldiers and servants, writers and musicians. The recently restored palace of Abba Jaffar, where the last king of the region lived, gives some idea of the fine style in which they lived.

We made an uneventful night stop in a hotel near the bus station. The next time I passed through Jima was not so uneventful however. Some friends of mine who worked in the Omo National Park had tried to drive to Addis via Maji, Dima and Jima, a route that is rarely used. It was the beginning of the wet season and when they reached the Akobo, a wide muddy tributary of the Blue Nile that drains the south-western Illuababor highlands, the river was in flood. There were a number of trucks parked on the riverbank waiting to cross. As the trucks could cross the river when it was still far too deep for a vehicle such as their Range Rover they struck a deal with one of the truck drivers to take their vehicle across on the back of his truck. This seemed like a great idea until the truck driver tried to cross when the river was still quite high and got completely stuck just short of the opposite bank. Heavy rain then fell in the highlands, the river flooded again and eventually rolled the truck over on its side with the Range Rover strapped to its trailer. The whole caboodle stayed like that underwater for a month or so before the flood subsided. At this point I volunteered to drive to Dima with my friends to help recover the contents of their Range Rover.

Dima, on the west bank of the Akobo, started as a Sudanese refugee camp, but has since sprawled into a large filthy village. It was here that I stayed in the most primitive hotel I have ever encountered. The walls were made of bamboo so that it was not only possible to hear everything that was going on in every room, but to watch it too. The beds had stiff straw mattresses and there were no bathrooms or toilets. In small countryside hotels I have come across some disgusting ablutions but I have never stayed anywhere with none at all. In fact, I discovered shortly after I arrived in the place that there were no toilets anywhere in the village. I was advised to get up very early in the morning and head out of town before everyone else did the same and hope to find some relatively pristine spot – not a pleasant exercise given that things had been like this ever since the town began and pristine spots were now few and far between.

We managed to unpack the marooned Range Rover, and with my car heavily loaded we started on our return journey to Addis, via Jima. At a road block just outside Jima, we were arrested at gun point, and forced to drive to Jima police station, a policeman with a loaded AK 47 sitting in the front of my car with us. As the reason for our arrest was a complete mystery to us we tried to argue with the police. But Mike, my friend, who knew a little Amharic understood them to say that we were definitely not going to be freed until we had been to the station. Once there, the police aggressively set about searching the car. They became more and more agitated and angry as they unpacked every box and suitcase only to find decomposing groceries, sodden stinking clothing and camping equipment and even a small rotting fish. Reluctantly, they finally gave up and let us go, though one police-man accompanied us to our hotel to keep us under surveillance. We passed a nervous night in Jima still none the wiser as to the meaning of it all, wondering what was going to happen next. Anyhow, nothing happened and the following day we arrived in Addis Ababa without any further trouble. The next day Mike spoke on the radio telephone to some Red Cross friends in Dima who told him that a self-appointed spy had watched us unloading the Range Rover and informed the police that he had seen us shifting gold from the car in the river to my car. While I can now dine out on having been arrested for smuggling gold I can't unfortunately produce any gold itself and neither as far as I know can Mike – though maybe he's just not letting on.

The next day our drive took us through Bedele, home of the

Bedele beer factory, Matu, and Gore to Gambela, where we arrived late afternoon. From Bedele the road passed through very thick forest and crossed several large rivers. The south-west highlands of Ethiopia, the wettest part of the country, boasts the most extensive indigenous forest left in the country and the road skimmed the edge of this area – a thick profusion of trees, tangled with vines, all dripping with moisture. In the past it must have been a paradise for animals. We were lucky to see some baboons, colobus and vervet monkeys, but I am sure if one spent some time exploring this forest one would probably see other animals, like forest hog and many different birds. But a stop here was not on our itinerary and we drove on making our way to Matu. Although Matu was surrounded by attractive forested hills, the town itself was very dull and we drove on another 20 kilometres through less dense forest than before, to Gore, in times gone by the capital of the old Illuababor province. Gore was very cold and wet, but as we had been on the road a good six hours we were feeling slightly peckish and stopped for lunch in a local hotel. The rain poured through the roof as I tasted my first Ethiopian national meal, *njera* and *tibs*. *Njera* is the Ethiopian national dish, a sour-dough pancake made from *tef* flour. *Tef* is a very interesting plant – an indigenous cereal unique to Ethiopia. Compared to wheat or barley it is shorter and wispier but its husbandry is similar to other cereals. To make *njera*, *tef* flour is soaked for several days in water until it starts to ferment. The *njera* mixture is then stirred well and poured little by little onto a hot griddle, often an old plough disc set over an open fire. It is cooked for a few minutes until brown before it is turned over to cook on the other side. In fact it is cooked in just the same way as an European pancake. It is pale brown all over when ready, and served cold with meat or vegetable sauces known as *wat*, or with *tibs*, small pieces of stewed beef or mutton, cooked with onions, spices and large quantities of chilli.

The steep escarpment from Gore down to the Baro River took us through a magnificent landscape of steep green valleys that reminded me of the Valley of a Thousand Hills in Natal, South Africa. I am sure the vegetation was quite different, but the rolling hills, green with tall grass, were very reminiscent. Having

11

completed the 1200 metre descent the chill in the air was gone and the atmosphere became hot, sticky and damp. We followed the Baro river to Bonga, a Sudanese refugee camp from where another hour's drive through acacia country dotted with rocky outcrops took us to Gambela.

Gambela was full of surprises. Within an hour of arriving at the hotel I was challenged to several rounds of table tennis by the Gambela National Park staff. It seemed to be a remarkable thing to be doing in the middle of nowhere. The next morning I was astounded to see the villagers bathing in the mighty Baro River, which was notorious for its large numbers of huge crocodiles. According to the town people this was a daily occurrence but they failed to say how many folk disappeared during these bathing sessions. The chance to have a drive in the national park accompanied by the warden and the biologist was also a surprise, a pleasant surprise, especially as there had been recent heavy rain, making roads wet and slippery – but with their assurance of a safe trip we ventured forth. A real surprise was in store for me here for I found the park, renowned for its swampy characteristics, to be full of rice and cotton plantations, and everything that goes with plantations like vehicles, villages full of human beings, and cattle. We drove as far as Abobo, a village 82 kilometres south of Gambela. The warden confirmed that the days of a remote national park were over and that as far as he could see, the only way to preserve any of the wildlife in the Gambela area would be to keep a small protected area in the furthest extremity of the park, east of Gog, which is another 80 kilometres south of Abobo. We did not see any sign of wildlife, but he assured me that there was still a small population of lechwe antelope surviving, and there were occasional reports of one or two elephants. He himself had recently seen lions. He also explained that many of the cattle and people I saw had slowly made their way across Africa from northern Nigeria; Fulani people, who, some years back, on arriving in the Gambela area, had liked the place and decided to stay. They now had up to 30,000 cattle in the park. Other visitors to Gambela, though I don't know if they ventured into the park, were the tall, black people from southern Sudan, who lived in the big refugee camp at Bonga which we had passed by 80 kilometres from the town.

Back in the days when rivers were arterial highways Gambela was an important river port linking Ethiopia to the Sudan and ultimately the Mediterranean. The Baro is a major tributary of the Nile and before the Aswan dam blocked the river you could if you wished sail your boat from Sydney, Australia direct to Gambela. In 1907 Gambela was established as a British free port and it became a popular trading destination with Khartoum. Coffee and grain (and no doubt ivory and slaves) were exported from Ethiopia to the Sudan and Egypt, especially in the wet season, when the river was high. It used to take seven days to travel down the river to Khartoum and eleven days to travel up. In 1936 the Italians captured the town. It was repossessed by the British in 1941, in 1951 became part of the Sudan, and finally reverted to Ethiopia in 1956. The port ceased functioning in 1974.

The altitude of the town is a mere 450 metres and it lies in a swampy, mosquito-ridden lowland, west of the Ethiopian plateau. On arrival, the town is not easily visible. Its two wide avenues of government buildings boast bright red flamboyant trees and purple jacarandas but they are hidden, along with groups of huts, in a hollow between the main road and the river. The town is inhabited by the Anuak and the Nuer people. The women are very colourful with a profusion of bead and other necklaces hanging down their bare breasts. The Anuak talk of themselves as 'bead people' and for them beads are a sign of wealth. Traditionally they fish and practise mixed agriculture. Some long-horned cattle are kept on the grasslands away from the river. The Anuak are generally very tall and dark-skinned. Smaller but even darker than the Anuak are the Nuer who, although they originated in the Sudan, are now more numerous in Gambela than the Anuak. They are all friendly, hospitable people as were all the folk we met in Gambela.

Our hotel, the government Ethiopia Hotel, was slightly out of town on the banks of the Baro River. We slept, ate and drank there except for our last night when we went to have a quiet supper at a popular local restaurant. By mid-evening the place was full and loud, rhythmic music spilled out of tattered loudspeakers. Our quiet evening turned into a raucous party during which we got to know a number of other Gambela visitors as well as local residents. Among others a group of UNHCR personnel partied with us until the small hours and we fell into our beds just before dawn to catch a couple of hours sleep before starting for Nekemte.

The next morning before dawn we took the road north to Dembidola, climbing up through a hilly area of dry, short grass. Dembidola is 137 kilometres from Gambela. The sun was just creeping over the horizon when we were overtaken by a UNHCR truck on its way to collect provisions for the Gambela refugee camp. Everyone on the truck had been partying with us during the night but they seemed wide awake and lively and waved at us enthusiastically. I felt quite the opposite and was having trouble keeping awake, so I flopped back in the reclining seat and slept for a couple of hours. It was going to be a long drive, at least 450 kilometres, to our ultimate destination, Nekemte.

Dembidola is 211 kilometres from the next town, Gimbi, and during this part of the journey we passed through an isolated area of harsh stony country where I saw a man in a brocade cloak and hat standing by a small rickety shed, ringing a bell. The cloak was full in style and hung almost to the ground. It was red and was patterned with gold thread. The hat was round with a flat top, and appeared to be made with black velvet. It could have been a Salvador Dali painting, it was such a strange scene. Here was a pale blue sky, and a sea of light grey rocks and boulders with hardly any vegetation stretching as far as I could see and in the middle of this there was this brightly coloured brocade-clad figure standing quite alone ringing a bell. I said to Cherent that he must be a madman. On the contrary, he told me, the figure was a Christian Orthodox church priest collecting donations from passers by. 'Maybe they are hoping to build a church somewhere in the area, but they are short of funds,' he said. Since that time I have seen many of these priests on every journey I have made but I have never been able to discover if they are all planning to build a new church in their area. If so, the number of churches is going to increase formidably. They

14

usually stand on an open stretch of road where they can be easily seen and where it is not difficult for cars to stop. Generally they are not too far from a town or village where they obviously go to spend the night. Once I noticed a priest ringing his bell just outside a town right beside two beggars. I wondered if the priest and the beggars weren't doing exactly the same thing and was it really what was expected of a priest? Other than the priest incident the day's journey was uneventful and we arrived in Nekemte shortly after dark.

When we arrived in Nekemte, the capital of Wolega Region, there had been a recent, quite unseasonal rainstorm there. The town was a quagmire, and the surrounding forest was alive with frog and cicada calls. We stayed in a double-storey hotel which, though fairly new, was already very shabby with dirty plastic dining room tablecloths being diligently picked over by hordes of flies. It was a most unpleasant place.

Unfortunately we arrived too late to look at what was touted as a very good museum with an interesting array of Oromo artefacts. All the same we were relieved to get out of the car and have a meal and a good night's sleep.

The next day about 80 kilometres out of Nekemte I noticed clouds of smoke pouring out from under the Pajero bonnet. The battery mounting had broken and the battery was lying on its side dripping acid onto the hot engine. It was a relief to find the problem was something comparatively easily rectified for my heart had missed a few beats when the smoking began as I thought the engine was on fire. Shortly after we got back on the road we had a puncture and then within the hour a second puncture. As we were carrying only one spare wheel, we couldn't go on. We were stuck in a very isolated spot with not a person, let alone a village, in sight. We sat on the roadside for what seemed a very long time discussing our plight and then a young lad came walking down the road and told Cherent that there was a village with a small tyre shop about four kilometres further on. He and Cherent set off on foot for the place, rolling the tyre before them, like a toy hoop, and I settled down on the grassy bank to watch over the car.

It was a magic time of year, early October. A cool breeze

rustled the grass, there was not a cloud in the sky. I had a Walkman with me and a sketch-book and charcoal so I settled down by the roadside to pass the time of day. I always carry a sketch-book but I have never yet used it. I have some kind of hang-up about sketching and drawing and find I can only do it if I'm sat at my easel in a studio, which is a terrible disadvantage for someone who has travelled so much. I remember my History of Art lecturer saying to us once that if you wanted to read Paul Klee's book *On Modern Art* it was not possible to do so lounging on a bed. It was the sort of book that had to be read when you were sitting at a library table wearing a suit. Maybe he had the same kind of problem with this book as I have with my sketching.

Within minutes of settling down wondering whether to try to sketch or just simply listen to the Walkman I was surrounded by young goatherds who had obviously heard the car stop and had converged on the spot leaving their goats to look after themselves. They had come to investigate and stare at the *ferenji*, (foreigner). In time they had the courage to sit beside me and we took it in turns to listen to the Walkman. Whilst someone was busy listening I opened up the sketch-book and asked one of them to draw a picture. I didn't speak Amharic but they probably didn't know very much either, as they would have spoken Orominia, the local language. So I mimed to them, rubbing the charcoal on the page and offering it to the child who sat nearest to me. The boy drew a house and he told me it was a *bet*, which, in fact, is Amharic for house. So I wrote that underneath the drawing and told them that in English it was a house, and I wrote that underneath as well. (Amharic with its ancient syllabary is the official language of Ethiopia, although some 80 other languages are spoken in various parts of the country.) Every child had a turn and eventually we had a whole page of pictures captioned in English and Amharic. Then an old man came along and shouted at them and they scattered back into the bush. I suppose he'd seen the goats abandoned and sent the children back to work.

A commotion on the road just out of sight, chattering and laughing, turned out to be Cherent coming back from the village. He must have been away about four hours. He was surrounded

16

by a group of youths, one of whom was rolling the tyre for him. Once that was back on the car our plan was to go to the village and have the other tyre repaired and then make our way to Bahir Dar. However, one of the youths told us that we were broken down very near to a state farm where there was an excellent garage, and we should go there for the second repair and at the same time have the battery mount fixed properly. We took his advice and drove down a track turning right off the main road through acres and acres of maize to arrive in a substantial farm village with garage, school, clinic, canteen and rows of houses.

This was one of the state farms opened during the Mengistu regime and it was still being run by the present government. Mengistu was the communist dictator who in 1974, with a group of fellow army officers (the Dergue), overthrew the feudal monarchy of Haile Selassie, following a series of demonstrations and strikes in the towns and land seizures in the countryside. The Dergue ruled Ethiopia for the next 17 years. Mengistu introduced many communist ideas to Ethiopia, including the establishment of collective state farms all over the country. The present government is gradually selling off the state farms to private investors, but this one outside Nekemte had not yet found a buyer.

Unfortunately the farm garage was closed for lunch but we were well entertained by the employees, in particular one old man who had been married to an Italian woman and had children and grandchildren living in Rome. He was very hospitable, spoke English, French and Italian, but I think spent his now lonely life thinking and longing for the past. He obviously drank a lot of beer, as he did that day, and when he became intoxicated he pestered us to take him with us and get him a job in Addis Ababa. I felt guilty leaving him behind when we finally left the farm and bade everyone goodbye. It was four o'clock in the afternoon by the time we reached the main road so we decided to drive back to Nekemte for the night, as Bahir Dar was still a very long way away.

The main event the next day was seeing the Blue Nile Gorge, a huge chasm which winds for 500 kilometres through spectacular grey, bare basalt, with occasional patches of thorn scrub, creating steep scarps for as far as the eye can see. The Blue Nile (known as the Abay in Ethiopia) arcs south of Lake Tana and then flows westwards into the Sudan, where it joins the White Nile near Khartoum. At over a kilometre wide and almost as deep the gorge is said to be comparable to the Grand Canyon. As a spectacle it is much harsher, lacking the warm reds and oranges of the Grand Canyon. The Blue Nile Gorge panorama is too large for the camera and anyhow the army forbids photographs in the area because of the strategic nature of the bridge. Just what purpose the ban on photographing Ethiopia's bridges serves is a typical Ethiopian mystery, for everywhere in Ethiopia tourists (and spies) can buy an excellent postcard of the bridge crossing the Blue Nile at Dejen. The soldiers guarding all the bridges are very jumpy and on this occasion our car was searched and everything turned out on the ground.

On a later trip I crossed the gorge on the bridge near Dejen, and that was quite a different story. Cherent and I were travelling with some friends from Uganda. We had been to Lake Tana and were on our way back to Addis. We drove over the Dejen bridge and climbed a fair way up the escarpment of the gorge when someone said, 'Let's stop and have one last look at the gorge.' We stopped the car and drew over to the side of the escarpment, looking down on the river. The bridge was just out of sight. We heard a loud commotion in the vicinity of the bridge and Cherent said, 'The soldiers are shouting at us.' The visitors yelled, 'No, they're shooting at us.' And indeed they were. Fortunately we must have been too far away or otherwise they were very bad shots for the bullets went wide. But what were they trying to do? This was pretty drastic action to take against a few tourists who couldn't even see the bridge from where they were, and the soldiers must have known that. We bolted back to the car and started up the escarpment at high speed. I have never been used as a rifle range dummy before and I hope I never am again.

Anyhow, this, my first day in the Blue Nile Gorge, was not as exciting as that, and once the soldiers had finished searching the car we left the place and several hours later arrived in Bahir Dar. The Ghion Hotel where we stayed in Bahir Dar was in a beautiful spot on the shores of Lake Tana. There was a very pretty garden which went right down to the lake's edge. Planted right in the middle of the garden was an extraordinary signboard forbidding anyone to take photographs of the garden without a permit from the hotel. I thought this was a very quaint idea at the time but the necessity for pointless permits while travelling round Ethiopia became the bane of my life and soon lost its funny side.

Lake Tana is the biggest lake in Ethiopia and its other claim to fame is that it is the source of the Blue Nile. The lake is dotted with islands supporting ancient churches and monasteries, some of which can only be visited by men. Just what cataclysm will befall the men if these men-only churches are visited by women, or where in the Bible provision for such institutions is made, I don't know, nor was I in a mood to find out that day. There are very many ancient churches to see in Ethiopia but I had not yet got myself into gear for church visiting, so on this trip we gave them a miss. Instead we hired a small boat and paddled around the lake for an hour or so. It was fascinating to watch the heavily loaded papyrus boats coming across the lake from the islands to Bahir Dar. On shore they looked so flimsy but in fact they can carry large loads of firewood across the lake in not always very calm weather.

It made a pleasant change to lounge around by the lake for a couple of days and we had a good walk at the Blue Nile Falls, some 30 kilometres south of Bahir Dar. The falls themselves were in full flood and a tremendous volume of water collecting from four separate streams was tumbling over the rocks to fall 45 metres down into a fairly narrow chasm. It was a stupendous sight which reminded me of Victoria Falls on the Zambezi River. Any mighty waterfall is breathtaking when in full flood.

We chatted to the local children who were selling much sought-after soft drinks and they told us the Amharic name for the falls, *Tis Abay*, which means Smoke of the Nile. They followed us down the grassy slopes, supposedly showing us the way which was, in fact, not a mystery. But they helped me to keep my balance as we clambered over slippery boulders on the steep incline down to the falls and I was pleased to have them along. It was a happy day, which was rounded off by a visit to a traditional nightclub. It was my first sight of live Ethiopian dancing and this club had an excellent variety show, with different dances from all parts of Ethiopia. It was both an enjoyable and educative evening. The most memorable dance was one performed from the Arsi and Bale regions of Oromo, when the women excelled themselves with several minutes of violent head twirling. How they didn't become giddy and fall over at the end of the movement was quite beyond me. In another dance from the Gurage region the dancers were required to clasp their hands and hold them out in front, while at the same time giving mighty kicks with bended knees out to the back, and all this to a very fast tempo. Tigray girls played drums during their dance which was much quieter, with dancers shuffling around in a circle for long periods of time, stopping at intervals to face a partner, and with hands on the waist, shake their shoulders in a fashion that looked for all the world as though the joints were dislocated. This shoulder shaking is the common feature in nearly all the Ethiopian dances, though it is probably practised most of all in Amhara dancing when the shaking takes on an incredible speed, causing women's breasts to gyrate, and the heads of male and female dancers to move back and forth at very high speed. An Ethiopian friend of mine calls these dances 'chicken dances' as the motion is reminiscent of the way a chicken's body seems to move independently of the head. Unlike other common movements seen not only in Ethiopian dances, but in Bantu and some European dancing, for example, stamping, hip thrusting and gyrating, scuffing, jumping, twirling, hopping and walking, the shoulder shaking is unique to Ethiopia. It requires tremendous concentration and effort, and the dancers, sometimes men as well as women, often hiss as they shake to stop themselves from getting breathless.

I found the dances fascinating and I thoroughly enjoyed the traditional music played on a *kebero* (drum) and a stringed instrument, either a *masenko* (one string) or a *krar* (six strings). However, I didn't enjoy the singing and I have never come to terms with the songs performed by the Ethiopian women. The notes are pitched very high and forced out with a kind of ululating wail that reminds me of the keening that takes place at Ethiopian funerals.

The office messenger in Cherent's office died a few months

after I arrived in Ethiopia and I attended his funeral. On arriving at his house I was ushered into the room where the coffin lay, and invited to sit down beside the dead man's sister. The room was crowded with women in national dress who chatted in low voices about everyday things. Without warning the sister, who had been conversing with the person next to her, launched into a piercing wail which was immediately taken up by the other women in the room. They then took turns singing eulogies to the dead man, punctuated at intervals with more keening. After 15 minutes there was silence and then everyone resumed talking in low voices. This unnerving performance was repeated several times whilst I was there. It was so mechanical I couldn't work out if people were really distressed, or if it was just their 'culture', as Ethiopians describe so many of their unusual habits. Anyhow, the Ethiopian female singers seem to have taken a leaf out of the funereal wailing book: mechanical, piercing, and unnerving.

In Bahir Dar we stocked up on tyres and bought two extra ones, good retreads. The road to Gondar and beyond was notorious for its sharp stony surface. As we drove towards Gondar the countryside was ablaze with the little yellow daisy known here as the meskel flower. The Ethiopian meskel ceremony celebrates the finding of the Lord's cross by Queen Elleni of Rome and the flower is called the meskel flower because it blooms at the time of the celebration. In fact the meskel celebrations had already taken place, but there was still an abundance of these flowers on the hillsides intermingling with lush green grass. Everywhere was a bright yellow and green patchwork. A group of donkeys carrying several bunches of meskel flowers on their backs reinforced the coloured patchwork as they were driven down the road by a farmer. We stopped to look at the donkeys and it was then that I noticed that on the other side of the road wild flowers of every description − pinks, purples, blues and different shades of yellow − were in profusion. Henry Dutton in his *Narrative of a Journey through Abyssinia in 1862−63* says of this same area:

Nature here appears always to put on a splendid robe, like a beautiful woman richly scented; for here the wild rose is more common than with us, and jasmine, honeysuckle and

21

other flowers abound; the number and variety of them covering the bushes and trees gave a gorgeous colouring to the landscape, that few artists would dare to put on canvas, for fear of seeming to overstep the bounds of truth.

Our visit to Gondar was not a great success because the royal compound with its high wall that encloses at least ten castles was not open to the public that day. The city was founded in 1635 by Emperor Fasilidas and became the seventeenth-century capital of Ethiopia, famous for its medieval castles and churches. When Fasilidas died in 1667, Gondar was the most important city in the empire with at least 65,000 inhabitants. Gondar remained the capital until the mid-nineteenth century. This period was considered the high point of Ethiopia's medieval culture and was a time when the arts flourished. After this the central monarchy gradually lost importance to powerful regional rulers. Today Gondar remains a large, impressive city. The name is derived from the words *gon idr*, which loosely translated means that you have to take shelter if you stay the night, because Gondar is renowned for its icy cold night wind.

However, on this occasion we didn't stop to familiarise ourselves with the bitter wind but simply made a fuel stop and took the opportunity to buy some cough mixture as Cherent had taken my cough and cold on board and was feeling pretty lousy. Our route would now take us via Debark and Shire to Axum.

I suppose I should have been disappointed at not being able to see the sights of Gondar but I was having such an interesting trip that I simply resolved to come back again one day. I have had to do this on many occasions in Ethiopia because people tend to take a day off and shut up shop as it pleases them with no thought for how it may disrupt others. As well as that, I have found that authorities in outlying areas are very high-handed and do as they please regardless of the inconvenience to the traveller or bona fide visitor. As an example, one weekend several months later I'd arranged to visit Magdala to see the battlefield where Lord Napier had fought the Emperor Tewodros. During Tewodros' reign, between 1855 and 1868, he had aimed to unify the country which had fragmented since the Gondar downfall.

But his efforts failed, partly due to his own growing unpopularity. He had tried to introduce a rule that each church should only have enough land to support two priests and three deacons, and that the rest of the land should be taxed like all other land. Church leaders disagreed with ferocious rebellions in Shoa and Tigray. At about the same time Tewodros asked Queen Victoria if he could send an ambassador to the UK. As she didn't reply he imagined that Britain was plotting against him along with the Turks and the Egyptians. In retaliation he took several British prisoners and imprisoned them in his hilltop fort at the top of Magdala mountain. Britain's attempt to negotiate the release of these prisoners failed, and so they sent a large force of troops to Magdala under the command of Lord Napier. Lord Napier also had support from the Tigray leaders. Tewodros, seeing that he was going to lose the battle, shot himself. Remains of his fortifications as well as his giant cannon are still standing there on the mountain to this day.

The mountain is a spectacular sight and it is only a day's walk or mule ride to the top from the small village of Tenta, about 550 kilometres from Addis. So I set off early on a Friday morning to Tenta, picking up Cherent on my way out of Addis. We spent our first night in Dese and left early on Saturday morning for Magdala. We planned to arrive in Tenta at lunchtime, get some mules and take off to camp half way up the mountain for the night. It was amazing, driving out of Dese on a Saturday morning, for all the farmers were coming into town for the Saturday market. I counted literally hundreds of donkeys and mules that day shuffling along under their heavy loads. Some of the animals were carrying unbelievably heavy burdens and, as is evident all over Ethiopia, the muleteers were not always very kind to their animals, which were frequently lame or had gaping sores on their backs. One day I was complaining to an Ethiopian friend about the terrible cruelty to all animals in Ethiopia, and I remarked that overseas animal rights people would be horrified if they could see the goings-on. My friend looked at me in astonishment. 'Animal rights?' he said in disbelief. 'Here we don't even have human rights.'

I thoroughly enjoyed the drive to Tenta, which was fortunate under the circumstances (one doesn't always have a good journey and the destination is what makes the day), for when we arrived in Tenta, we were simply turned away. This was a perfect example of what Robert Louis Stevenson had in mind when he famously said that 'It's better to travel hopefully than to arrive'. He could have been on this very trip. 'Do you have a permit?' the police demanded. 'What permit? Why do we have to have a permit? Who should we have got it from? Now please be reasonable, we've driven two days just to climb Magdala and now you tell us to go back to Dese and get a permit? When did this rule come into force?' But they had no answers, nor were they going to let us pass. We couldn't go back to Dese and then back to Tenta again because we hadn't the time. Besides, who knows, we might not arrive with an acceptable permit the second time. So we returned to Addis Ababa, certainly a little hot under the collar.

The Magdala fiasco was not the only such absurdity I've encountered. In fact, the longer one spends in Ethiopia the more often one finds the right hand at odds with the left. I have been unexpectedly turned back at three other places I've tried to visit. I went once to Dila, a little beyond Awassa on the road to Kenya, to look at the famous monoliths. Not only had I a good description of the stelae themselves but I also had a detailed description of how to get there. I slept a night in Awassa and arrived in Dila mid-morning next day. I thought it would be polite to tell the local government tourism and culture department where I was going. I also suggested that one of them might like to accompany me because lack of transport hampers government travel every-where in Ethiopia. In fact it was quite the wrong thing to do. They were unfriendly and rude and forbade me to go anywhere near the place, without the courtesy of an explanation.

The same thing happened on a visit to Melka Kouture, in the great Rift Valley near Butijira. It is a world-famous fossil site where many remains of early man have been discovered. The fossils have been exposed where over the millennia the Awash River Gorge has cut through layer upon layer of ancient sediments. At the entrance to the gorge a large number of tools, shelters and traces of meals have been found at many of the higher levels. In the lowest levels pebble tools were found, and in the layers above, middle and later Stone Age men have left double-edged hand-axes and obsidian scrapers. Fossil bones of hippo, rhino, elephant and various antelope have also been dug up. It is a fascinating place and having spent time in many other fossil sites I was looking forward eagerly to seeing Melka Kouture. But having gone all the way there I was refused entry to the enclosure, again, because I did not have a permit. It's always a puzzle to me what conceivable difference the permits make and it's certainly a puzzle to guess where one might get them. Why does one never hear about them until one's arrival at a place after the completion of a long journey?

Another frustrating journey was a trip I made to Mount Zequala. This mountain is a huge volcanic cone all by itself in the surrounding plain about 40 kilometres from Addis. It stands 600 metres above the plain with a crater two kilometres in diameter at the bottom of which is a lake of holy water. Juniper forest covers the inside of the crater rim creating a cool, peaceful setting. I had already been up this mountain once before and passed a splendid day picnicking and walking around the little crater lake. On the second occasion I'd brought along some Ethiopian friends who had never had the chance to come before. There is an Orthodox church at the top of the mountain and I knew my friends would enjoy visiting that too. This time we picnicked near the church and then set off down to the lake. Halfway down the track we were stopped by a most obnoxious little man who said that women could not go any further down the track because the lake water was holy and if women went down there it would dry up. I asked how that could be, considering that I had been all round the lake last year – as had many other women – and as he could see for himself the lake was still there, full of water. It made no difference. Logic plays no part in religious men's view of the dangers to sanctity posed by women. He just laughed and shepherded us back up the hill. On the way home the car broke down – proof perhaps of the Almighty's displeasure at our presumption in questioning the priest.

Anyhow, back on the road to Axum we found ourselves struggling with punctures again. By the time we had travelled half way to Debark, still a long way from Axum, we had already had four punctures and were completely stuck again. This lesson taught me never to buy second-hand tyres and to always carry patches and tyre levers in the car. It is so easy to mend a tube and so difficult to find help on the road.

Fortunately a bus came our way and this time we decided that Cherent should wait with the car and I would take a tyre on the bus as far as Debark, some 55 kilometres, get it repaired, and find a lift back. The Simien Mountains National Park office was in Debark, and as I was carrying a letter of introduction to these people from the director, I hoped that they would give me a hand. Cherent said they were more likely to help me than him. I think though that his real reason for suggesting I go was quite different. He knew that at that time of year on the farms in that area he could find fresh broad beans and *tella*, a rough traditional beer brewed from barley, for a very cheap price. I was right because he told me later that whilst I was battling with punctured tyres he spent the day lying in the grass by the roadside eating beans and drinking *tella*.

The national park staff were very friendly and arranged for me to have the tyre repaired at once. It was very fortunate for us that they had a vehicle going to Gondar within an hour of my arrival in Debark and I was invited to ride back in it to our crippled car. At this stage I was beginning to wonder how much further we could go without more tyre problems and I decided it was time to buy new tyres. The driver of the park Land Rover said he would do that for me in Gondar and bring the tyres back with him in about four days time. We finally got to Debark late that evening. Now we were three in the car for we had hired a scout, Marelengne, from the park people to travel with us just in case we had any more problems. We told him our story of woe and how we would be in Debark for four days waiting for our new tyres. We were wondering what we were going to do during that time. 'Well, visit the Simien Park,' he said. This was a great idea which had not been on our itinerary.

The Simien Mountains National Park lies on the western side of the Simien mountain range, one of Africa's largest mountain ranges, which boasts Mount Ras Dashen, Africa's fourth highest peak. The western plateau falls away 1000 metres on both the north and east sides creating precipitous escarpments from which you can look over the vast plains of the Great Rift Valley. The hills at the foot of these escarpments are eroded into bizarre-shaped pinnacles and buttresses. This mountainous country is home to three of Ethiopia's most famous endemic animals – the walia ibex, the gelada baboon and the Simien fox.

We joined the scout, Marelengne, and his mule driver, Tshage, and set off to the park the next morning. It took some arranging at such short notice as we had no camping equipment or food with us. However, everything worked like clockwork. We borrowed two ancient igloo tents and two very thin sleeping bags and went off to Debark to buy onions, potatoes, rice and tins of meat. Tshage turned up with four horses – one for Cherent, one for Marelengne, one for me and one for one of the Simien Park experts, Derevey, who had joined us. He also had two mules to carry our gear. Since this first trip to Simien with Tshage, Marelengne and Derevey I have been there three more times and always been lucky to travel with the same crew. Marelengne was not only a jack of all trades, but a master of some too. He was a first class cook and on every trip he organised the meals with the skill of a cordon bleu chef. He was an expert horseman, able to make any stubborn mule behave like a good Arab horse. He was also a good mechanic and an excellent marksman. In jest we would ask him if he was also a good husband. He never answered that question.

Tshage was a priest. He had a special way with the horses and mules, unflappable and gentle and he was alert and attentive to any inexperienced rider, ready to chase after you and get you back on the track if the mule had decided to take an alternative path. This was not uncommon when the mules came to a junction in the track, one path leading onwards and the other going to their home. All of a sudden your hitherto listless animal would take off at the double in the direction of home but before long you'd find Tshage sprinting alongside, scolding the animal and catching hold of your reins. He had a horse of his own. It was a pretty tan colour with a black mane; a small, quiet horse which he used for ploughing when it was not out on a trek.

Derevey was a kindly, serious man, always with a pair of binoculars slung around his neck and usually wrapped in a volum-inous *gabi*. A *gabi* is an open weave cotton wrap measuring

27

about two by one metres worn by just about everyone as a shawl against the cold weather.

The park trip was unforgettable. Although, as I said, I have since been there three times, the first visit will always stick in my mind. It was a completely new experience for me. I have never trekked in high mountain ranges before, apart from a few short sorties out of Zermat, Switzerland, into the Alps in springtime. The rolling Simien highlands were not unlike the Zermat slopes. Mount Ras Dashen at 4620 metres is just 200 metres higher than the Matterhorn, which towers above Zermat at 4474 metres.

On the first day we set off through the Debark market and travelled at a good pace across fields and a river. Everyone was riding except Tshage. He walked because Cherent and I were amateur riders and to start with he led us on a rein. He didn't find it difficult to keep up with us. All too soon as far as I was concerned, for I was enjoying the ride, we had to dismount to scale a very steep hill which the local people call *kazera*, meaning walking stick, a reflection of how difficult the ascent is. It took us three hours to reach the top after which the track was easily negotiated on horseback. This was an area of rolling hills, with villages and farmers ploughing. That shook me for we were supposedly in a national park where ploughed fields were hardly what we expected to find. Since that time I've learned that all of Ethiopia's national parks are occupied by people and that all are in a precarious state of preservation because of it. Early on in our ride we saw a large troop of gelada baboons, strange looking monkeys with a big red heart-shaped patch of bare skin in the middle of their chests. This odd feature led to the old belief that the animal's breast had been ripped open to display a bleeding heart and gave rise to their common name of 'bleeding heart'. The males in particular have huge manes that function as raincapes a very useful adaptation for life in the cold, wet mountains. The gelada was the first of Ethiopia's endemic mammals that I saw.

It was exhilarating breathing the mountain air, sometimes walking, sometimes riding. Farmers' children approached us to sell us their woollen helmets which sat snugly on their heads, covering their foreheads and ears, styled like the helmet a charioteer used to wear. This headgear smelt strongly of farmyard for the wool was not cleaned, just spun and woven in the huts. But they soon lost their odour when continuously exposed to the fresh air.

We arrived at our first camp at Sankaba just after dark. It was a bitter night and I wondered how Ranulph Fiennes, the famous Antarctic explorer, could stake out on an ice cap and then sleep. Our igloo tents were very old and extremely thin, and so were the sleeping bags. I hadn't realised that a chilling wind would start to blow during the night making it even colder. I had no warm clothes with me, not having planned to make this trip, but I did have a bottle of whisky. After many gulps I curled up in my bag and tried to sleep. It was so cold. I do not remember having been so cold in all my life and I barely slept. It was a relief to see first light at around six when I left the igloo to take a brisk walk around the camp to try to get my blood flowing again.

I discovered that we had camped in a truly magnificent spot, unnoticed when we arrived because it was dark. Sankaba was on the edge of an escarpment and I found myself looking down on a panorama of green, strange-shaped hills and mountains, steep valleys and sheer scarps – all completely still and silent. I had to pinch myself to persuade myself it was real. What a truly marvellous spectacle it was – something very special. Rosita Forbes wrote of this spot in 1925 in her book *From Red Sea to Blue Nile*:

> The most marvellous of all Abyssinian landscapes opened before us, as we looked across a gorge that was denuded amethyst to the peaks of Simien. A thousand years ago when the old gods reigned in Ethiopia, they must have played chess with those stupendous crags, for we saw bishops' mitres cut in lapis lazuli, castles with the ruby of approaching sunrise in their turrets, an emerald knight where the forest crept up on to the rock, and far away, a king crowned with sapphire, and guarded by a row of pawns.

The second night's stop at a place called Chenek was even more spectacular, for here there was a view in every direction. We were sitting on a heavenly pinnacle, able to observe a hundred peaks, slopes and cliffs. Two lammergeyers that circled our camp had their nest in a nearby cliff. The lammergeyer, or bearded vulture, is one of the Old World's largest and most localised carnivorous birds. Its numbers have been reduced drastically in recent decades and Ethiopia is one of the only places left where you still have a good chance of seeing one. The lammergeyer has a very specialised way of feeding. It favours bone marrow which it gets by scavenging bones. It then carries the bones high over a suitable rock surface dropping them onto it to smash them open and expose the marrow. We saw a lammergeyer take a bone from near our camp but unfortunately it didn't smash it open near enough for us to see.

A short ride from camp we peered over another precipice to look for walia ibex on the cliffs hundreds of metres below us. We peered for ages into the distant haze, scanning every likely spot, but we never saw an ibex. Marelengne swore blind he could see two perched on a flat rock about 200 metres below. We gazed hard at the spot he indicated but if he could indeed see them we certainly couldn't.

Nowadays the best the visitor can hope for is to spot an ibex at the limit of human vision for they only now survive well out of reach of rifle shot. Jill Last in her book *Endemic Animals of Ethiopia*, puts it graphically:

Forced by man to retreat, and to retreat again, [the walia] has been driven in its extremity to inhabit the most inaccessible cliffs of the Simien escarpment. The walia once existed in significant numbers, probably several thousands, in the highland massif, feeding on the cliff faces and coming up to roam the plateau at rutting time. Large herds wandered unmolested on these chilly heights.

She wrote this in 1982. In 1997, the walia population was estimated at a mere 560 animals.

I prepared myself well for the second night by collecting dried grass to make a mattress on which to spread my sleeping bag. Then, at supper time, when the fire was burning hot, I selected a big, solid rock and warmed it in the fire. When I went to bed

I wrapped the hot stone in a towel and wedged myself around it in the sleeping bag. It worked a treat as a hot water bottle and I slept well all night.

On a later trip accompanied by one of my daughters we slept three to a tent in order to keep warm. It was indeed cosy and we barely had room to move. Pig-in-the-middle slept in line with the centre pole with a person on either side and although this was a tight fit, the space was guarded jealously for it was the warmest place in the tent. One night my daughter had pole position. Suddenly in the middle of the night she sat up and shouted accusingly 'Ma, you're at the pole.' Lying half asleep I couldn't figure out what was going on or what 'at the pole' was supposed to mean. She said it again, this time with a powerful shove and a kick that realigned me in my allotted space. I realised then that in my sleep I had successfully manoeuvred myself into pole position.

I felt quite melancholy on the trek back to Sankaba, passing through moorland dotted with giant lobelia and red hot pokers, to spend our final night. We took a different path through an area which was lying fallow and so we saw no people at all. I enjoyed the quiet isolation of the place, and it gave me a sense of what the Simien mountains used to be like. At one point on the journey Cherent's mule stumbled on the stony ground and Cherent fell off. It gave us all (except Cherent) something to laugh about. It wasn't a bad fall, for his animal was very short and stocky and so Cherent didn't have far to tumble.

On our arrival in Debark I felt as though I had been 'everywhere' and it was an effort to find the enthusiasm to continue to Axum. However, with new tyres on the Pajero we felt that at least there would be no more puncture problems on the road which was something of a relief. All the same it seemed the high point of the journey was, quite literally, behind us and I found myself reluctant to leave Debark. As we left the town early the next morning the road became very narrow with what seemed a hundred hairpin bends as it dropped 2000 metres down into the foothills of the Simien. This remarkable piece of road engineering was carried out by the Italians who at the time had probably not envisaged that the road would be used by 12-metre long buses or heavily laden trucks with trailers. I was not surprised to learn that during the rainy season sections of the dripping walls of the carved out road were apt to collapse and put the road out of action for weeks.

We were making good time on the road between Debark and Axum. It was thrilling to be down in the valley, looking up at the Simien mountains, and even though we were at a lower level we still had plenty of small escarpments to climb and little rivers with pebbly beds and absolutely clear water to cross. The day grew hotter as we neared the Tekeze River valley, and gradually the Simien chill thawed out of our bones. The escarpment down into the Tekeze is almost as spectacular as the Blue Nile Gorge, though not as big. It must be a great deal dryer for the scenery is brown and sandy and it is very hot. The Tekeze River has its source in the mountains near Lalibela, east of Lake Tana. From there it flows north and meets with a tributary that originates in Lake Ashangi, a pretty lake that you pass if you are driving from Mekele to Alamata in eastern Ethiopia. From the confluence the Tekeze flows on north and then turns west where it eventually joins the White Nile.

The area was deserted apart from some soldiers guarding the bridge across the Tekeze into Tigray. The river is the boundary between Gondar and Tigray. Arnold Toynbee, in his book *Between Niger and Nile* regards the Tekeze river as a much more important frontier. He says, 'Tigray, like the rest of North Africa, belongs culturally to Western Asia. In fact the frontier between Asia and Africa is delimited, not by the Suez Canal, but by the gorge of the River Tekeze'.

As we began the climb up the escarpment into Toynbee's Asia on the other side of the river there was a terrible smell of burning. It was the clutch plate, and as it burnt out we came, for the third time, to a complete halt, in probably the most isolated spot so far. We sat by the roadside for at least an hour and a half, ears straining to catch the sound of an approaching vehicle in good time so that we could be ready to flag it down. But there were no vehicles. A wandering cattleman joined us and Cherent arranged with him that if a car did come, but would not tow us, we would leave him guarding the Pajero whilst we took a lift to the nearest sizeable town – Shire – to find help. We didn't really expect any vehicle to tow us up the hill, but we did hope to get a lift. The town's real name is Inda Silase, but locally it is known as Shire, after the name of the district in which it lies. It was a bit of a risk to make such an arrangement with an unknown wanderer, but there was little else we could do. Generally, rural people are very helpful and trustworthy and glad of the welcome cash for their services. It was lucky we'd made this plan for no sooner than it was settled than we heard a heavy vehicle grinding its way up the escarpment. We hastily locked the car, leaving some biscuits and the jerrycan of water for our *zebegne* (watchman), telling him we'd get back as soon as possible. The vehicle proved to be a bus and two hours later we arrived in Shire.

It took hours to find someone willing to tow our vehicle up the escarpment to Shire. After many unsuccessful enquiries we finally made an arrangement with a matatu taxi driver to do the job. I hated the idea of doing this at night, but the matatu driver was only willing to do it then because his daytime work was already spoken for. I was very worried about the dangers of towing the car round the steep, sharp bends in the dark, but I tried to reassure myself that this local man probably knew the escarpment like the back of his hand. What little confidence I had evaporated on the way down to the car for the driver went like a lunatic, slamming brakes on hard at every bend to stop us from tumbling over the edge into the precipice below. I got some comfort from the Elton John music playing on my Walkman, and also from the fact that I knew he would not be able to travel so fast towing the Pajero uphill. Nevertheless, it was a nightmare dragging the vehicle up the escarpment with the towrope snapping several times and the taxi engine overheating. We all really only stopped to breathe once the machine was parked in a Shire garage at about one o'clock in the morning.

There were no spares in Shire and the garage mechanic advised us to buy a new clutch plate in Addis Ababa and send it to him. That would mean leaving the car behind, taking the plane to Addis and then coming back with the spare part. It seemed like a bad idea, because Cherent's leave would run out before the exercise was complete. Besides, when we made enquiries about available seats on the plane to Addis there was as usual a long waiting list for the next two flights. After much deliberation, and because I was keen to follow our road even if I could not stop wherever I wanted to, we decided to take the bus from Shire to Addis. We planned to buy the spare part in Addis and send someone back to Shire on the bus to repair the car and drive it home.

We left Shire on the bus at five o'clock the next morning and were in Axum in what seemed like a very short time. We didn't stop there for more than a few minutes but as we crept through the quiet streets Cherent pointed and said 'That's the way to the stelae field and the Queen of Sheba's pool. King Kaleb's Palace is up that hill. Here is the Axum Museum and St Mary of Zion church.' And that was about it as regards my first sightseeing experience of Ethiopia's most famous historical place. From the bus it was of course not possible to see any of these places and all I could do was resolve to come back another time.

Axum is the oldest city in Ethiopia and it was the capital city from around the first to the seventh century A D. It had contacts with Nubia, Egypt and Greece at this time through its port on the Red Sea coast, Adulis. The Axumites were a literate people. Their most powerful king was Ezana who ruled with his twin brother in the fourth century. He was converted to Christianity which he made the official religion. Axum boasts a large field of carved stone monoliths or stelae dominated by a 23-metre high block of granite that was transported from a quarry nearby, probably by elephants. This stele is attributed to King Ezana himself. The stelae of Axum are not of any religious significance but are supposed to demonstrate the power of the ruler who constructed them. The largest of the stelae, attributed to the third century King Ramhai, now lies in pieces on the ground. It was probably ruined by the Judaic Queen Yodit, who during her drive to wipe out Axum and Christianity in the ninth century, destroyed many monuments and churches.

Another important Axumite king was Kaleb who ruled for 30 years in the sixth century. King Kaleb does not have a stele to his name but the ruins of his palace can still be seen on a hill about two kilometres out of town. On the way up to this palace you pass a dam known as the Queen of Sheba's Pool, said to have been built for her, though it is some distance from the ruins

34

of her palace, built on the present day outskirts of the town. In Axum's St Mary of Zion church the Ark of the Covenant is supposedly kept under lock and key. The Ark of the Covenant was made by the Children of Israel to hold the Tablets of Law given to Moses by God on Mount Sinai. After the Jews settled in Jerusalem, the Ark was enshrined in a temple built by Solomon in 1000 BC. After the destruction of the temple in 587 BC it disappeared. It was brought to Ethiopia, so the story goes, by Azariah, the first-born son of the high priest of the temple of Jerusalem. Priests at the Tana Kirkos monastery on an island in Lake Tana say that the Ark was kept there for 800 years before King Ezana transported it to Axum in the fourth century. No one is allowed to see it in its hiding place in St Mary of Zion church. There is an excellent museum in Axum that holds many antiquities and provides information about the history of the city and surrounding country.

On the road from Axum to Adigrat we passed the 2700 year-old ruined city of Yeha, which has a well preserved 12-metre high stone temple said to be 2500 years old. Some distance from there we saw the turning to Debre Damo, where the monastery is famous for its sixth-century stone church, named after its founder, Abune Aregawe. It sits on a 3000 metres high cliff. The only way into the monastery, which is still in use, is by climbing a 15 metre leather rope, which hangs down over a sheer cliff. On 21 October every year there is a ceremony at the monastery when hundreds of people visit the place in remembrance of Abune Aregawe. 'The ceremony of the busy rope,' joked one of our bus companions who was obviously having trouble imagining such a large number of people going up and down the cliff to the church on a single rope. Abune Aregawe was one of the nine Syrian monks who in the fifth century carried on preaching the Christian word that King Ezana had ordained should be the official religion of his kingdom.

On route to the Debre Damo junction we had already driven through Adwa, surrounded by strangely shaped mountains, reminiscent of some of the Simien formations. Emperor Menelik II had defeated the Italian army at Adwa in 1896, in a battle celebrated in Ethiopia as the greatest African victory against foreign aggressors, though I thought the thrashing the Zulus gave the British at Isandlhwana was just as memorable. We stopped for lunch in Adigrat having driven up the mighty sandstone Debre Damo escarpment with its terrifyingly steep and narrow hairpin bends. This drive seemed much more dangerous than when we were on the escarpment from Debark for now we were actually *in* a 12-metre bus, not just thinking about it. After the escarpment we travelled the long, dusty, potholed road from Adigrat to Mekele to stop for the night.

Ever since leaving Debark I had noticed a radical change in the architecture of the rural houses. In these parts they were oblong and built of stone, with a flat roof, mudded, and frequently with grass growing on them. This was Tigray architecture and many of the houses were difficult to see because they were built up against a hillside of the same colour stone. On the road to Mekele I knew we were driving through an area where many ancient, small churches were also built into rocky, Tigray mountainsides. At the time I had no idea where to look out for them and even if I had I assumed that they would be too well hidden to be seen from the road. On a later journey when I did visit some of these churches I found that my assumption was correct. They were not meant to be seen easily, to protect them from attacks from other religious groups especially the Muslims.

We spent a night at Mekele. Although Mekele is a small town it is the capital of Tigray. It is a modern place developing fast, though it still harks of older times as one can frequently see long camel trains passing through the town on their way down into the awesome sandy Danakil to transport salt back to the highlands. The bus stopped and dropped off some passengers near the Mekele market where we saw some of these salt traders unloading their camels. They had arrived, and so had we. I was thinking about how remarkable it was that the bus, carrying 70 passengers, had travelled the 330 kilometres from Shire to Mekele in a day, with only one driver. The road was rough and the driving must have been tiring. In many countries there would have been two drivers on board this kind of public transport and they would have taken turns to drive.

At least half of the people on the bus had tickets to Addis

Ababa from Shire, so we got to know each other well, and, like at school, we bagged seats for each other, not letting newcomers invade our space. The bus played music throughout the journey. This was turned up to full volume as we approached towns and villages, presumably to draw attention to our arrival in case anyone wanted to board. Some of the people on the bus were from Tigray and others were from areas around Addis Ababa and so there was plenty of competition for which cassettes should be played. But everyone was happy and arguments were gentle and lined with humour. Or so I supposed, for I could not understand a word anyone was saying, but Cherent confirmed my supposition. People ate a lot of sugar cane during the journey, as well as bananas, and oranges, and some people chewed *chat*, a green leafy stimulant introduced to Ethiopia by the Muslims. All pith, skins and stalks were thrown onto the floor of the bus, so by the time we reached Addis Ababa it was as though we were travelling on a mobile rubbish tip. But it didn't really matter because people were talking and laughing and singing, and, as the Ethiopians would say for this kind of communication, 'playing' with each other.

The second night we spent in Dese, the capital of Wollo. It is a dirty place, spread along a valley with high mountain ranges on either side. To get there we had dropped down 1000 metres from Mekele to Alimata on yet another escarpment where the driver at one point found it very difficult to manoeuvre the bus. He entered a hairpin bend too sharply, coming round the inner curve only to find the bus would not make it round. He seemed to hesitate, wondering whether to try to continue forward hoping to make it without falling off the edge of the cliff, or to back up and make extra room to manoeuvre. This was the only time on the bus journey when I lost confidence in the driver and became extremely frightened. While he hesitated I stood up, and trying to appear calm, though I was far from it, said that I should like to get off. This was evidently exactly what all the other passengers felt too, for when they saw me move to leave they followed suit. This mass exit made the driver's mind up for him and he chose to back the bus up. He completed the manoeuvre successfully and we all climbed back in and started a new song.

These escarpments are hazardous for inexperienced drivers

and as is so often the case with nervous drivers, they fail to slow down and shift into low gear before starting the ascent. Rather, they attack the climb by going as fast as they can hoping to stay in a higher gear and not have to change. But, inevitably, the vehicle loses momentum and the driver has to change down on a steep, rough slope. Having made things much more difficult for himself than they already were he is apt to miss the gear or stall, end up in neutral, start to roll backwards and set the stage for helpless panic, often aggravated by indifferent brakes. Many tales are told of horrific accidents from just such a scenario. Another hazard, common on the escarpment before Dese, is fog. On another occasion I was travelling late in the evening on the Dese escarpment. It was a particularly black night, with heavy fog. It was quite impossible to see the twists and turns of the road and I felt the only thing to do was to stop the car and sit it out. However, my cousin, who lives in the fogs of Scotland, suggested that he run just in front of the car and lead the way. In this way we made it five kilometres through the fog and arrived in Dese without mishap. Shortly after, we learnt that a bus had plunged over the side on this same stretch of escarpment, killing everyone on board.

Between Mekele and Dese we passed the road to Lalibela, where in the twelfth century King Lalibela constructed the now famous rock churches. The churches are in two clusters, separated by the Jordan River, so named by King Lalibela after a visit to Jerusalem. The eastern cluster comprises seven churches and the western cluster five. The ones on the east are mostly completely underground, carved vertically down into the bedrock on relatively flat surfaces. Several of them are monoliths or three-quarter monoliths, isolated from the surrounding rock on all or at least three sides, a style of construction unique to Ethiopia. The churches of the western cluster are similar to many of the Tigray churches, being excavated horizontally into vertical rock faces by exploiting natural caves. One of the churches in the eastern cluster, Bet Medhane Alem, is said to be the largest rock-hewn church in the world and because of its style it is thought to have been modelled on the original St Mary Zion church built by King Ezana at Axum in the fourth century. It is not known how many people were involved in the building of the Lalibela churches. Estimates range from 40,000 craftsmen and labourers to just a few people assisted by angels.

After Dese we passed the turn-off to Mile. Along this road you can visit the busy market at Bati, well known as a meeting place for northerners and Afars from the east. The market attracts thousands of people selling grain, cattle, camels, clothing, silver jewellery, salt and many other commodities. Further along the same road, quite near the junction of the Bati and the Mile road, is the turn-off to the site near the Awash River where the famous 'Lucy' was excavated. Lucy, or, as she is known in Amharic, *Dinkinish*, meaning beautiful, is a female australopithecine skeleton between 3 and 4 million years old, at the time one of the oldest known pre-hominids. Since the discovery of Lucy an even older fossil has been found 80 kilometres south of her, dated at 4.4 million years old. This fossil of *Australopithecus ramidus* is the oldest of man's ancestors ever discovered and is regarded by some experts as the legendary missing link between man and the apes. At a later date I came back and tried to visit the place where Lucy was found, but I was turned back by the police. At least on this occasion instead of demanding the usual mysterious permit they said the reason was because the nomadic Afar and Issa tribesmen were fighting and there was a risk I might get caught in the crossfire, something I was happy to avoid.

On the third day at about two o'clock in the afternoon we arrived in Addis Ababa. It was a Friday, a fasting day because Orthodox Christians abstain from meat on Fridays. At lunchtime we had stopped in a town in the hills, called Debre Sina, where I was introduced to *shurru*. This is an Ethiopian fasting food, or *wat*, made from ground chick peas or lentils mixed with chilli sauce. Little did I know at the time that I would spend several days in Debre Sina on another occasion when my car broke down. On this occasion, though, we reached Addis without mishap. The next morning we contacted a mechanic and gave him the money to buy a new clutch plate, plus his bus fare to Shire. Cherent went back to work. My mother rang me from the UK. 'Where have you been?' she said, 'I've been trying to contact you the whole week.' I laughed. 'I've been everywhere.'

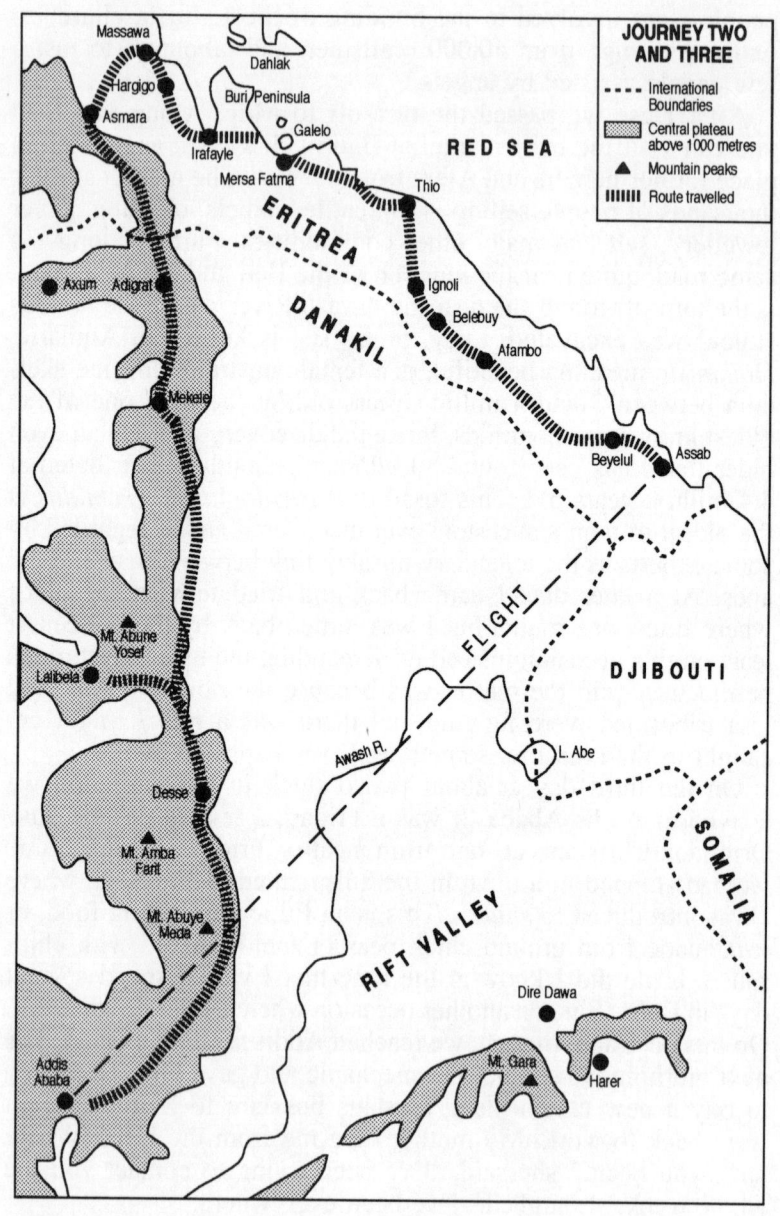

2

A Burning Tablecloth and a Fallen Tooth

In April 1996 we decided to drive to the port of Massawa, on the Red Sea coast of Eritrea. From there we planned to try to reach the port of Assab, 725 kilometres to the east by the track that starts off along the Red Sea coast and then cuts inland through Denkalia, from all accounts a forbidding desert where not many travellers go. 'The desert of Danakil is a part of the world that the Creator must have fashioned when he was in a bad mood': so says Ladislas Farago in his '*The Busu Tshiki-Tshik*', in *Abyssinian Stop Press*, 1936. However, I had heard that a weekly bus had started to do the trip so I figured that if the bus could make it so could we.

First of all I had to obtain a visitor's visa from the Eritrean Embassy. Cherent didn't need one because he is a citizen of Ethiopia. The visa was dealt with in a very prompt and efficient manner and the Eritreans had it ready for me in 24 hours. They were extremely polite and friendly people at the embassy, who made me feel somewhat ashamed of my own embassy, whose staff are arrogant and unfriendly to foreigners applying for visitors' visas to visit the UK.

We started the trip on my birthday. We had had a hot celebration the night before, and I mean literally hot, at one of the three-Star hotels in Addis Ababa. The birthday dining table was laid out to perfection with a pretty, green, scallop-patterned cloth laid over a fresh white tablecloth. There was a profusion of flower and candle decorations and some hotel-made oil lamps that gave a soft, cosy light. We ate a scrumptious main course and then

41

with plenty of ceremony the waiter brought the birthday cake heavily laden with candles. I really cannot remember exactly what happened next, but having put the cake on the table, I believe he decided to top up the paraffin in one of the oil burners. At the same time another waiter came to light the candles on the cake. Paraffin was spilt, a lighted match dropped and within seconds the green scallop tablecloth was alight. It turned out to be made of plastic and a black, gooey mess started to spread over the table keeping the flames burning brightly. There was a tremendous commotion, beating out the flames, removing the cake so that it wasn't spoilt, the waiters all very serious, and the birthday guests doubled up with uncontrollable laughter. What I had to decide was if this was a good or bad omen for the forthcoming trip!

Anyhow, the next morning Cherent and I set off in my short wheelbase Toyota Land Cruiser. It is always enervating starting a trip and I was happy to be driving my own car instead of a hired one. Our route took us to Debre Birhan, Debre Sina, Robit, Senbete, Dese, Mekele and Adigrat (backtracking the bus trip that I had been forced to take when my hired Pajero broke down five months earlier) and then over the border into Eritrea. The road past Debre Birhan (well known for its woollen carpets and blankets) is spectacular as one is able to look down on vast gorges carved out by the tributaries of the Blue Nile. After that the road climbs up to ascend the slopes of Mount Termaber whose summit is at about 3250 metres. There are three tunnels to pass through during the ascent of the mountain, the 587 metre-long Termaber tunnel and then two smaller ones. As one leaves the third tunnel one is faced with a magnificent view of the Rift Valley 2000 metres below. From here the drive is downhill, through Debre Sina and into the Rift Valley, past Robit and Senbete. Senbete is a very lively town on Sunday mornings because a big market is held there. Three different tribes converge on the place, the Argoba, the Gile Oromo and the Afar, bringing a wide selection of goods with them for sale: grain, cattle, clothing, silver jewellery, chickens, camels and salt. This market has become increasingly popular with tourists who customarily used to visit Bati market.

The little car went like a bomb, though the suspension in the early model Toyota was very hard, and any bumps, holes or undulations in the road made the ride quite tiring. On this journey the road between Debre Birhan and Dese was badly in need of repair as it was full of holes. Not just little holes dotted occasionally over the asphalt surface, but huge depressions and craters that joined up and spread everywhere, making it almost impossible to drive at any speed. I have heard people say that confronted with such a road surface they let their tyres down and drive like hell so as to avoid the discomfort. It didn't sound like a very sensible idea to me and I hadn't the courage to test it. Anyhow I see that I wrote in my diary that the road was f— awful. I must have become very irritable and I was probably driving too fast because at one point we hit an almighty bump and we took off into the air, coming back to earth a few metres further on. Cherent had been taken completely by surprise and had bounced up and hit his head on the roof and knocked one of his teeth out. This was not a very good way to start a trip: a burning tablecloth and a fallen tooth.

On the way we took the opportunity to divert to Lalibela having had to pass by on our previous trip by bus. We drove in via Woldia, Dilb and Kulmesk. Woldia, an ordinary little hillside town, is visited by a lot of tourists who are passing through on their way to Lalibela. Dilb, more of a village than a town, is built on the junction with the Kulmesk road and the main road, the magnificent escarpment road which links Woldia with Gondar. This road, a fine example of spectacular engineering climbing very steeply up the hillside to a giddy height, was built by the Chinese. There is a mighty drop into the valley below. Fortunately the road is very wide and the asphalt is smooth, but there are no crash barriers along its outer edge. If one is at the wheel one hardly dares to glance sideways.

Having turned to the right at Dilb, we found the next part of the road not good. Not only was it wet but it was also extremely rough. A couple of months earlier we had heard that a vehicle had broken down in one of the steep river beds that we had to cross. Before it could be recovered a heavy storm in nearby hills caused a bore of water to sweep down the river taking the car with it. This was a common event 30 years ago in East Africa, but nowadays, with more bridges, one doesn't hear of it happening so often. (Since we made this first trip the road between Kulmesk and Lalibela has been greatly improved to complement the upgrading of the airfield at Lalibela.)

One of the most hazardous features of the road was the little irrigation ditches that the farmers dig across the track at regular intervals. If you didn't notice these sharp, deep little trenches in good time and slow down, the vehicle took a terrible pounding. We found one vehicle on the route that had obviously taken too much punishment. It was an apparently abandoned Mercedes four-wheel drive, complete with camping equipment on the roof-rack and the inside full of goods and chattels. We enquired of some people living in a hut nearby where the owner of the car was because the car looked as though it had been parked in the same spot for a long time. They told us that the car belonged to some German tourists who had broken down the year before. They had hitched a lift out to the main road asking these villagers to look after the car until they returned. But they had never been back.

The hard drive across the irrigation ditches eased off as the road followed the beginning of the Tekese River as it carved its way through rough, mountainous country. There had been some recent rain and the going demanded a lot of gear changing and concentration. It was with some relief that we arrived at Lalibela, the little mountain-top town with its double-storey, circular stone houses. Lalibela, famous for its rock churches, is an extraordinary place. What struck me most was how these huge churches carved out of solid rock, some of them ten metres high, each had their own distinctive characters, shapes and decorations. The churches on the east of the (Ethiopian) River Jordan give the impression that they were conceived of as a whole whereas those on the other side of the river seem to have a more singular conception. The churches are used today as regularly as they were eight centuries ago, when the famous Zagwe ruler, King Lalibela, built them. The services are probably little changed though some of the customs surrounding the entry to the churches seem to have relaxed a little. For instance, at the beginning of the century only

44

men were allowed into the church of Mariam. In *From Red Sea to Blue Nile* Rosita Forbes writes:

> Into Mariam, the church of the Virgin, with a lack of logic that is truly Abyssinian, only men are allowed. 'Why do you exclude women from the one church dedicated to a woman?' I asked the Chief Priest, who was attended by an acolyte with a fly whisk. 'It is the rule,' he said. 'What would happen if Mary appeared on earth, and wanted to enter her own house?' The man of learning laughed. 'That is a very good joke! We should know her, of course,' he answered with the simplicity of a child.

However, maybe the clergy had second thoughts about whether they would recognise her or not, for nowadays the church of Mariam, thought to have been the first church built in Lalibela, is open to everyone. Some of the churches were stifled by horrible scaffolding with corrugated iron roofing erected to protect them from rain water that was leaking through cracked rocks. No thought appeared to have gone into the appearance of these conservation measures. It was an eyesore and something of an insult to King Lalibela and his team, who, with a few simple tools had managed to build one of the wonders of the world. Eight centuries later, with all the world's modern technology, an abysmal structure had been knocked together to protect it.

A mob of aggressive old beggars hounded us as we visited the churches. They asked us for a coin as we passed them, crippled and immobile, near the main entrance. I was amazed to see the same people two or three more times during our church tour, always crippled and immobile, but in different spots on the tourist route. They must have had some short cuts, that, immediately we were out of sight, they took to get themselves in position, prostrate on the ground, as we passed by again. If we refused to extend our charity they pulled at our clothes and abused us. We had paid a substantial entrance fee to the churches and I thought the recipients of that fee, whether it was the church or the government, should by now have made an arrangement to keep these beggars at bay, as King Lalibela probably would have done.

On our way out of Lalibela we took a different route, going straight on from Kulmesk to the main Dese-Mekele road instead of turning right to Dilb and Woldia. This was a pretty drive through terraced farmland, but the road was narrow and very slow, and we took four hours to drive the 120 kilometres. After that we had to charge up the main road in order to reach Mekele for the night, arriving, very tired, at about nine o'clock.

The next day was heavy going too, for the Mekele-Adigrat stretch of road was not yet tarred and it was very rough. We hadn't noticed this on our earlier trip by bus, but in the little car we felt like a couple of pebbles in an empty baked bean can. It was bliss to arrive in Adigrat in the late afternoon, find a hotel, have a meal, and sleep for a good 16 hours.

Adigrat is the second largest town in Tigray, after Mekele. It is a busy, friendly place surrounded by mountains and on the junction of the roads leading to Axum, Mekele and Asmara in Eritrea. On our way to Adigrat we had wondered whether to stop in Wukro or Sinkata to explore some of the Tigray rock churches, but we decided to press on to the Red Sea coast. Tucked away high up on sheer escarpments, some of these little (compared to Lalibela) rock-hewn churches may have been carved as early as the fourth century A D, predating Lalibela. In 1868 when Lord Napier was on his way to Magdala to fight Emperor Tewodros, he passed through the small village of Wukro, where he was shown a church carved into a rocky outcrop. For a long time after that it was thought that this was the only church of its kind in Tigray but gradually more and more have been discovered and documented and nowadays it is thought they number more than 130.

We felt refreshed the next morning after a good night's sleep and set off for the Ethiopia-Eritrea border post in high spirits. On arriving at the border we were mortified to see at least three large bus loads of people queuing for customs and immigration formalities and we suspected that we would have to spend the best part of the day waiting our turn. However, all the officials worked at a remarkable speed. I supposed they were accustomed to this heavy traffic between the two countries. In no time at all it was our turn and so we passed into Eritrea in good time and without any problems.

Eritrea became an independent country in April 1993, after a 30-year war of secession from Ethiopia. Eritrea has a long history of subjugation. The Italians colonised the country in 1898 and remained there until 1941 when they were defeated by the British in the Second World War. A British military administration then governed Eritrea until it was federated with Ethiopia in 1950. The first organised opposition to Ethiopian rule was that of the Eritrean Liberation Movement.

The country is bordered by Sudan to the west and Ethiopia and Djibouti to the south. To the north and north-east is the Red Sea, bordered on its other side by Saudi Arabia and the Yemen. It covers an area of 124,000 square kilometres. Eritrea, like Ethiopia, uses the Julian calendar with twelve months of 30 days each and a thirteenth month of five days. The Julian year ends in the first week of September of the Gregorian calendar used in the West. The Julian calendar also runs seven years and eight months behind the Gregorian calendar. The reason I have been given for this lack of synchrony is that the wise men, having visited the new-born Christ, took seven years and eight months to reach Eritrea and Ethiopia to tell them of the birth. On hearing the news the beginning of the first century A D was declared.

Most Eritreans living in the towns and bigger villages speak Amharic because during the country's federation with Ethiopia the traditionally-spoken languages of Tigrinya and Arabic were banned as official teaching languages in favour of Amharic.

On our way to Asmara from the border post we drove through kilometres of harsh sandstone and sometimes red-soil country with mountain escarpments and wide views. The landscape was littered with numerous small, round buildings, frequently painted in bright colours. These were modern Christian Orthodox churches whose conventional architecture contrasted sharply with the descriptions I'd been given of the rock-hewn churches we had left behind in Tigray.

Asmara is at an altitude of 2347 metres on the eastern edge

47

of the central plateau. Due to the Italian occupation, the central part of Asmara around Liberty Avenue is quite European in character with its broad tree-lined boulevards and outdoor cafes. The village of Asmara was known to Venetian travellers as early as the fourteenth century, and this original village is now contained within the north-east part of the city. On the whole the city is very quiet compared to Addis Ababa. There are no donkeys or sheep in the streets and there are no beggars. Hotels are numerous and we had no difficulty finding ourselves rooms. We stayed in the Shegay, and though it was being refurbished everything ran very smoothly. It was very attractively decorated with house plants on all the outside landings. It was also central – a useful feature because we had to visit the Road Transport Authority to get a permit for the car to re-enter Ethiopia by a different route. The licensing officer at Road Transport was astounded to hear that we planned to take the Red Sea route to Assab. He said he had never before heard of a *ferenji* wanting to drive from Massawa to Assab. Anyhow, he persuaded us to go to the tourist office and buy a copy of the map he had hanging on his wall. He then gave us our permit and wished us well. We took his advice and bought the map. The information it gave us about our route to Assab from Massawa seemed fairly accurate, but there was not enough detail on it for first-time travellers in that area. With this lack of information we decided that we would feel happier doing the journey if we could go in convoy with the bus. Most of the bus drivers on that route, we'd heard, had been drivers in the area during the war for independence and so they were well acquainted with each and every sand dune.

The next morning we found that the main escarpment road between Asmara and Nefasit was closed for maintenance. This meant travelling back up the main road to Dekemhare to take the old road to Massawa for the first part of the descent. This old road was not asphalt, but we had plenty of time to enjoy the slow 40-kilometre drive. There was very little growing in this parched area, until we reached Nefasit where we saw a small vineyard, and from there on for the next ten kilometres the hillsides were green. The old road does not have the steep escarpments and panoramic views of the new road. Between Asmara and Nefasit the new road winds through dozens of hairpin bends with dizzy drops of 250 metres on either side of the road to the valley floor. The barren peaks are frequently not visible because of heavy mist and the journey can be very cold.

We joined the new road at Nefasit and crept down to Dongollo where the going became faster because the country was not as steep. We planned to spend two days in Massawa by the sea, swimming and resting and preparing ourselves for the desert onslaught. Dongollo is just over halfway to Massawa from Asmara and spurred by the thought of two days at the sea I put my foot down and within the hour we drove into Massawa. We made for the Gurgusum Beach Hotel, a little way out of town. Whilst we were registering a German woman asked Cherent if it was safe to swim in the sea. Had all the mines been removed? Such present-day hazards of Eritrea's recent history had not entered my head. I was glad to hear the receptionist assure her that no mines remained and that the sea was clean and ideal for her children as it was shallow for a long way out. I found it just as the receptionist described it.

The island port of Massawa has been consecutively occupied by Turks, Egyptians, Italians and British and the mixed architecture of the old buildings bears witness to these occupations. It's a charming town. When it cools off in the evenings the place livens up and the little alleyways between the Turko-Egyptian and Italian buildings begin to bustle with people. The town is something of an oasis in the desert coastal plains.

Lying from 15 to 110 kilometres from Massawa, the Dahlak Islands, famous for fishing, snorkelling and diving, number around 200 and are scattered over a wide area in the Red Sea. The coral reefs in the area are supposedly second to none in the whole world. We didn't have time to involve ourselves in water activities and busied ourselves instead by buying provisions, a spare fan belt, a couple of jerrycans of water, and fuel. We visited the bus station to find out when the bus would be leaving, but nobody had any idea. Evidently the bus came from Asmara and as it never left Asmara until it was full there was in effect no schedule. In view of this we decided to set off alone the next morning.

I was slightly apprehensive as we drove out of Massawa the next morning. However, I felt much better when a man flagged us down and asked us for a lift to Hargigo, ten kilometres from Massawa, where he wanted to visit relatives. As we drove along he told us there was the ruin of a 150 year-old mosque in Hargigo but other than that the town didn't have any redeeming features. We didn't stop to see the mosque, but when we dropped the man off we were pleased to pick up another man who wanted a ride to the next town, Foro, 48 kilometres further on. At this stage I was imagining that we would probably have a passenger with us for the whole journey and that thought calmed my nerves no end.

The road to Foro cut inland. Its hard surface was very stony and dusty and the surrounding country was dry with a good deal of thorn scrub. It smacked of what was to come. Our plan was to try to reach Thio on the first day, 305 kilometres from Massawa and 420 kilometres from Assab. Once we were in Thio we would make plans for day two and, if necessary, day three.

Foro had a very large dam just outside of the town that was being used for irrigation. Before the war with Ethiopia, Foro had been a major agricultural centre and it seemed as though there were plans to make it a productive centre again. The town also boasted its proximity to the ancient port of Adulis, nowadays popular for archaeological excavations. Adulis has another claim to fame, too, in that it was near the place where Lord Napier landed when he brought his troops from England to fight with Emperor Tewodros at Magdala in 1868. From his landing near Adulis Napier and his force of 32,000 men and some elephants walked to Magdala. This was an amazing journey of about 700 kilometres through the north of Denkalia into Tigray, passing through the then small village of Wukro, where they saw the rock-hewn church, and then up onto the plateau and on to Magdala. What a remarkable effort, just to release a few British hostages.

In Foro we dropped our passenger, and as luck would have it picked up a third man who wanted to travel to Irafayle. The driving time from Massawa to Irafayle was about four hours. It seemed much more. Driving through unfamiliar country always seems to take a long time, but, in fact, we arrived in Irafayle at about ten-thirty that morning, and when we stopped there to have a soda, we congratulated ourselves on our good progress.

Irafayle means elephant pasture but there are no elephants to be seen there these days. The small village marks the beginning of the Buri Peninsula with its wide, sparkling bay, and large sand-spit. However, getting from the small town to the bay was no mean feat and this stretch of road was the worst I have ever travelled on in all my life. The road was very steep and it appeared that it had just been carved out of the hillside, leaving all the fallen rocks and boulders to form the road surface. We crawled along at a snail's pace. At every jerk of the Toyota I expected to get a boulder through the petrol tank. I worried constantly if this was how the track to Assab was going to be, because if it was, it would take us many weeks to reach our destination. I began to feel apprehensive again, especially as no one in Irafale had asked us for a lift to the next village, Galelo. We took about two hours to drive this short but steep rocky escarpment and on arriving in the bay we stopped, hot and flustered, to have a snack out of our rations and a long drink of water. The cliffs behind the bay were alive with baboons and a klipspringer jumped up the hillside when it saw us climbing out of the car. The sea sparkled bright blue and in the distance we could see the Dahlak Islands. It was a welcome rest, after which we took the road to Galelo, crossing the peninsula west to east. This was a sandy stretch of road on which we made good time, although in one area there was a stretch of very wet sand and I was sure we would get bogged down. But we didn't and we arrived in Galelo, the administrative centre for North Denkalia, to hear that the bus was just ahead of us as it had spent the previous night in the town. I was elated because I thought we would be able to follow its tracks, but I soon discovered, driving out of Galelo, that there were many different tracks going in every direction. The army had several camps in the Dankalia and many of the tracks we saw were made by their vehicles. It was very confusing and it took us at least half an hour to find the correct road out of Galelo.

Whilst in the town we asked if there was anyone who wanted to travel with us to Thio but the bus must have picked up all the travellers as there were no takers. So we continued alone. I was panicking a bit now because we still had a long way to go before nightfall. It was uncomfortably hot and I wondered if the radiator would boil or if some other part of the car would break. In spite of all these anxieties I was riveted by the beauty of the 47-kilometre drive from Galelo to Mersa Fatma. The landscapes changed from fields of great purple boulders stretching as far as the eye could see to thorn scrub interrupted by huge tidal lagoons, to flat white sand stretching to eternity. All these scenes were set against the twinkling blue of the ocean. The merciless desert was so beautiful to look at.

Mersa Fatma used to have a railway line that brought potash from Dallol in the Danakil Depression to the coast for export through its harbour. However, there was little to be seen there now and it was hardly recognisable as a village at all. As we drove past Mersa Fatma with about 100 kilometres to go to Thio, the sun was gradually veiled by a light haze. It was only four o'clock in the afternoon and all being well we would be in Thio by dark. The haze grew denser and we realised that a sandstorm was blowing our way. Slight as it may have been then we figured that if the haze became even thicker it was quite possible that the track would be lost and then we would have a real problem. I slammed my foot down on the accelerator and flew along the track that passed through kilometres of featureless sandy country. We drove on through the sand for an hour, eyes straining for the right road. Then as we passed through a small village I almost ran into a small boy crossing in front of us for he was hardly visible in the haze. We were lucky not to hit him. Shortly after this, very slowly, the haze started to clear and I felt a great sense of relief. It was a pretty evening, about five-thirty, and the evening light made the desert sand look pale grey and cool in contrast to the shimmering white of the hot sand during the day. We were both looking forward to arriving in Thio and being surrounded by people. We had had enough for one day of the quiet harsh desert and its isolation.

Just after six o'clock we were excited to see some huts just ahead of us and we drove into a small village. We had arrived. A few villagers came out to greet us. There were no more than

15 huts to be seen and no shops or bars in the village. A few small boats, one with an outboard motor, bobbed up and down on an incoming tide. There was no beach to speak of, just stinking blackish mangrove mud. This couldn't be Thio. We must have taken the wrong track. We questioned an old man who laughed uproariously before telling us that Thio was a great distance from his village. But – if we paid him – he would show us the way. We couldn't believe it and I felt like sitting down and crying. But there was no time to cry as a long heated discussion among the villagers had started about how much they would charge to take us back to the right track and about which villager would be our guide. Finally we agreed on 50 birr and the old man was chosen to show us the way. But although Cherent wanted to go right away I had had enough for the day. It was nearly dark, and if we had missed the track by day, who knows where we might end up driving by night. I knew that Cherent felt nervous about spending the night in this village for some of the inhabitants looked far from savoury. I wondered myself how safe we were or if they would rob us. However, I insisted to Cherent that we should try to spend the night. Even if we didn't sleep, it would be good to lie down. When we asked them they agreed and in fact seemed delighted so I had no further misgivings. They made us tea and brought us two sleeping mats to put down by the car.

I rushed off towards the beach and the sea where I was looking forward to having a good splash. An old turbaned man rushed after me and gesticulated, intimating that I shouldn't go there. I stopped in my tracks, wondering if it was a men's holy place, like the lake at the top of Mount Zuquala near Addis. Why shouldn't I go there? I was looking forward to a swim. He mumbled '*shintabet*', one Amharic word I did know, meaning toilet. Did he want me to go to the toilet before I plunged into the sea? No, he was telling me that the villagers used the beach as a toilet and it was therefore very unhealthy to swim there. I pondered over this extraordinary habit of fouling the beach and taking away the one real pleasure one could have living in a place like this.

Disappointed, I walked back to the car where Cherent was surrounded by youths who were delighted to have someone from the outside world to talk to. They were asking him a lot of questions and he was asking them plenty too. What we wanted to know most of all was why these people should want to live in this tiny, godforsaken village by the sea you couldn't swim in. They appeared not to do any fishing, for there were no nets or other signs of such a livelihood. There was no vegetation anywhere around, just sand. They had no livestock. They were 45 kilometres from the main track to Thio and Thio was about 40 kilometres from that. Finally one of the older men enlightened us. He said that they transported young Eritrean and Ethiopian girls across the Red Sea to the Yemen. That was why the village was there. We didn't question him any further. Were these girls going of their own free will or was this some kind of slave trading? We didn't find out. As I lay down on my mat to sleep I felt mightily glad that I was a middle-aged woman and not a girl.

In the morning Cherent and I discussed what we should do in view of the fact that we had gone so far off the track. Once we had rejoined the main track we would have done, with all the driving around looking for the road in Galelo, an extra 95 kilometres. We didn't know if we were going to be able to buy fuel in Thio, and we didn't know either if we were going to get lost again. The fuel we were carrying would be enough to get us to Assab if we weren't able to purchase any *en route* as long as we didn't get lost again. We both felt intimidated by the long journey ahead of us. With a network of army tracks in the sand we realised how easy it would be to go wrong again. If we took the wrong road and then had the misfortune to break down it was quite possible that we could be lost forever to die a grisly death in the desert. I had always felt that if we had a serious breakdown we could get a lift on the bus, but this wouldn't be possible if we weren't even on the right road. We decided we should go back to Massawa. It was a disappointing decision, but I knew it was the right one.

An old man from the village travelled with us to the junction where we had missed the road. It was in the small village where we had nearly hit the boy crossing the road in the sandstorm. He had taken our attention for a split second and in that time we had taken the wrong track. The track that we had followed, so the old man said, was the water tanker track. Many of the isolated villages in the area were supplied with fresh water from the nearest big town by tanker. The track that we'd followed had been very well marked by the tanker's weekly visits.

And so we retraced our tracks. The drive seemed much less arduous on the way back and we saw some wild animals along the way – three ostrich, eight gazelle, one hare and a jackal. We spent the night in Massawa, and then drove to Asmara where we changed our permit at the Road Transport Authority so that we could go back into Ethiopia the way we had come. We didn't see the man who had advised us to buy the map. The road to the village that we had visited certainly wasn't on the map. As we sped towards the border post we vowed that we would make the trip again in the not too distant future, maybe not by car, but on the bus. We felt very lucky not to have had a major breakdown in the desert and laughed at our adventure. The trip back to Addis was uneventful until we reached Debre Sina. Having bounced across the million potholes again on the Dese road, but this time with a much weaker car because of the rough going in the desert, the Toyota had had enough. Just before we reached the town there was a big clunk from the back of the car, and then another clunk. Both of the back springs had broken clean in two. We waited in Debre Sina for two days until someone came from Addis to tow the car home. 'By the way, Cherent,' I said as we sat on the Debre Sina Hotel veranda waiting for the tow truck 'What was the name of that village where we spent the night?.'

'Bedada,' he said.

'What does that mean?'

'Fuck', he replied.

3

Mrs Fat and Furious

One thing that I've noticed since living in Ethiopia is that the people are absolutely obsessed with washing their hands and rinsing out their mouths. When I was studying dance at university I learnt that one of the reasons for learning dance in the old days was to promote good, clean thinking. A healthy body leads to a healthy mind. Rosita Forbes comments in *From Red Sea to Blue Nile* 'I decided that many Abyssinians are honest with money, none with their thoughts'. Maybe all the washing of hands and mouths is an unconscious cleansing of guilty thoughts and deeds. Whatever the reason, on my next journey to the desert this washing obsession could have cost us all our lives.

The Muslims travelling with us were much more realistic about water. When they saw how little there was they very sensibly washed their hands, feet and faces with sand before kneeling down to pray. The Christians on the other hand fecklessly kept on using the bus's water supply to wash with, oblivious of the risk of it running out. As onlookers to these rituals Cherent and I were very glad we'd taken the precaution of carrying a five-litre jerrycan of water plus a water bottle, both of which we kept well hidden when we realised which way the wind was blowing. When we'd boarded the bus in Assab the driver had assured us that we had no reason to worry about anything. He carried a 200-litre drum of water for a journey that took a maximum of three days, which, he claimed, was obviously plenty. It seemed equally obvious to me that that meant less than a litre per person per day which strongly suggested that a personal water supply was in

Blue Nile Falls. It was a stupendous sight.

Although the Meskel celebrations had taken place there was still an abundance of Meskel flowers on the hillsides.

A heavenly pinnacle in Simien Mountain National Park.

Derevey, Marelenge, Cherent,Tshage.

Senbete market.

Meskel celebrations,
Addis Ababa.

The Christian Orthodox church boasts all its splendor at the Timket ceremony.

Fields of purple boulders on the way to Mersa Fatma.

A wide tidal salt pan in Dankalia.

Every now and then a lone camel walked by in the desert.

A huge strangely shaped mountain standing isolated on the desert horizon.

The Afambo restaurant, a higgledy-piggledy construction, was made from mats.

Afambo stone houses camouflaged against the rocky hillside.

The afternoon sun was blazing down and even the camels hid in the shade.

The scenery changed dramatically after Belebuy when we were faced with huge, sultry, bare mountain ranges.

At Ignoli I watched goats drinking at a water trough near a well.

order. Sure enough, by the end of the first day we had covered a mere 260 kilometres of the total of 750 and the drum was already half empty.

But I'm ahead of my story, so let me go back to the beginning. It was exactly a year after our first abortive attempt that we decided to travel along the Red Sea coast again, this time the other way round, from Assab to Massawa. Our initial failure to reach our destination as the result of losing our way and ending up in a small village about 45 kilometres west of Thio had made us determined to try again. This time we decided to go by the bus that makes the journey every couple of weeks or so. The anxieties of the earlier journey had distracted us from appreciating the beauty of the coast and I looked forward to sitting back and concentrating on the spectacular scenery while the bus driver battled with road and machine.

We flew to Assab from Addis Ababa. The flight was about an hour and a half in a Fokker Friendship and the latter part of the journey took us over the flat bare rocks and lava fields of the country bordering the Danakil Depression. By road its a 14-hour drive from Addis to Assab. The 860-kilometre asphalt highway passes through Awash, Gewane, Mile and Serdo and is busy with trucks hauling goods from Assab port. For the drivers it is a lonely two-day journey of which more than three-quarters of the way is a desert of sand, basalt rocks and fresh lava with the constant threat of ambush by bandits. Just before Serdo there is a turn-off that leads to Asaita, 50 kilometres from the main road. Asaita is the capital of the Afar region, a hot, dry, dusty town where everyone keeps the heat at bay by drinking a lot of beer and sleeping outside their houses. It is not far from here that the mighty Awash River disappears underground, never to be seen again.

We found Assab a very dreary city, unlike earlier descriptions of it as a bustling seaside town with a modern port. Since Eritrea's independence from Ethiopia the port is much less used with a large proportion of Ethiopian goods now being imported through Djibouti and Kenya. I was looking forward to taking a walk along the dock to watch the ships being loaded and unloaded. There is always a sense of excitement at a busy dock with ships bringing goods from faraway lands and exchange goods being loaded to go to these unknown destinations. I had heard it was easy to get a permit from the port office at the dock entrance gate. As soon as we had checked into a hotel and bought our bus ticket for the bus leaving for Massawa early the next morning we strolled down the hill from the town to the dock gate.

'We'd like to walk along the docks and look at the ships,' I said to the guard at the gate. Please could you give us a permit?' He looked at me quizzically as though he hadn't understood a word of what I had said and so Cherent spoke to him in Amharic. The guard then called two other men and we explained to them that we wanted to wander around the docks.

'Oh, you must go to that small house over there and get your permit,' they said, pointing to a little brick building with a red roof. So off we went. A fat, angry-faced woman was seated behind a tiny desk in one of the offices in the small brick building. We asked for a permit, but she snarled that she didn't issue permits. 'You must go to the port authority in town.' 'Phew,' I said to Cherent, 'do we really want to walk along the docks?'

'Come on,' he said. 'We have nothing much else to do. Let's try it.' So we climbed back up the hill to the town and visited the appropriate office. This was a different place altogether with delightfully friendly and helpful staff. I began to think it had been worth it after all and we would soon have our little permit. The office messenger took us to see the head of the port section. He laughed when we told him what we wanted. 'Why have you come to me?' he said. 'It's not necessary. Just go down to the dock gate and ask the guard to give you a permit. He will let you through.'

'Come on,' said Cherent, 'Don't give up. Let's try again.' Cherent has been playing this game all his life and has a patience and optimism far beyond mine. Back at the dock gate the same guard called the same two men who again insisted: 'Oh you must go to that small house over there to get your permit.' Another confrontation with Mrs Fat and Furious was more than I could stomach so we gave up and went shopping. I wondered, as I had so often before, whether they knowingly play this game for laughs, falling about in helpless mirth as one leaves the office on a hopeless journey. But humour seems to be wholly absent. The essential element is the refusal, often spiced with a dash of anger, as in the case of Mrs Fat and Furious. I could see that, stuck in a dump like Assab as an essentially superfluous official, dealing with the tedium might lead one to come up with some tortuous solutions.

We had booked rooms in the Hotel Kebel opposite the bus station, to facilitate what was bound to be an early morning departure. When we visited the station in the early evening to confirm the departure the driver told us that we wouldn't be leaving until the day after next because not enough tickets had been sold to make the journey worthwhile. They would wait an extra day until the bus arrived from Ethiopia, as they expected to pick up ongoing passengers from that bus.

In many ways I was glad to have the extra day at our hotel because it was very comfortable and lively. It attracted not only Assab residents and visiting businessmen, but also sailors from the docked ships. The hotel night-watchman kept himself busy shooing away the professional town ladies who kept up a constant siege of the premises. An old man with a stick was no real deterrent though and at the table next to ours there were two girls talking with a couple of ship's crew, one man an Indian the other a middle European. I listened in on their conversation which proved quite intriguing. The men were trying to persuade the girls to accompany them to Australia describing the wealth and happiness they would arrange for them there. The girls were sceptical and laughed them off, presumably being well used to such dodgy schemes. The Indian sailor became quite impatient and thrust two Australian visa application forms in front of them and told them not to be fools but to fill them out. All they had to do, he said, was to apply for a three-month visitor's visa to Australia. He would organise things once they arrived in Australia and hey presto they would be able to stay there forever. It was just the entry formalities that had to be fixed. Just exactly where he intended trading them I hated to think.

Listening to them I was tempted to join the meeting to ask the sailor to do a deal for us. Only five months earlier we had invited Cherent to spend a two-week holiday with us at our home

59

in Australia, but the Australian High Commission in Nairobi had refused point blank to give him a visa. We were obviously not going through the right channels. But Cherent said he didn't want to spend the rest of his life in bondage in Macau or wherever so we left the girls and the sailors arguing about the pros and cons of emigration to Australia.

Boarding the bus two days later turned out to be a test of brute force. Mere possession of a ticket counted for little. Fortunately the driver spotted Cherent and I in a losing battle as we fought our fellow passengers for a seat where it was possible to take photographs through the window. He beckoned to us to board through his front door, which was very gallant of him, and we thereby took possession of the seat behind him.

It was a relief to be settled on board. As I watched each of the other passengers skirmishing savagely to get on the bus in front of all the others I wondered why they didn't just make an orderly queue and climb on peacefully. It was not as though they wouldn't all get on. Although the bus was supposed to carry only 70 passengers I knew it would carry many more if necessary. It was not in the nature of things for someone to actually be refused entry on the mere grounds of numbers. In fact, once the battle was over, there were 85 people on board.

The refusal to queue is common in Ethiopia and Eritrea — something to do with striving after food in the famines many people are all too familiar with? I don't know. When I first arrived in Addis Ababa I found myself in a very disorderly queue at the post office. Every time it was my turn to be served, someone pushed in front of me. Finally, when a very sophisticated-looking woman shoved me aside to get to the counter, I accosted her, saying, 'Excuse me, but it was my turn next. Why do you all have to push?' She smiled and said condescendingly, 'Why don't you push?' Thus invited I did just that and shouldered my way back in front of her. She didn't dispute it. The law of the jungle had prevailed, and everything was normal.

I once sat next to the same calibre of woman in a small restaurant in Abse Teferi. She and I were both travelling by bus from Harar to Addis and we'd stopped for lunch. I ordered a soda water and sat back to absorb the local atmosphere. She sat at a table not far from me, slim, well-dressed – altogether very elegant looking. She ordered *tibs* and when it arrived she picked at it like a duchess, taking dainty mouthfuls and chewing slowly. All of a sudden she crunched on a piece of gristle and in a sudden fury dragged the offending chunk of meat from her mouth and flung it to the ground, all daintiness forgotten. The elegance is so often very superficial. Cherent remarked that her lapse of ladylike manners was probably because she was a Recently Wake-up Woman. What on earth, I wanted to know, was a Recently Wake-up Woman? Well, he said, you often see them in the fashionable coffee parlours and restaurants of Addis. Typically, they are the owners of small-town *bunabets* (coffee shops) who've made a bit of money. They come to the big smoke to learn how the fashionable women dress and behave. You can tell them easily, he said. They wear flashy new dresses, imitation gold jewellery and too much perfume. But their awkward gestures and country accents are the real give-away. You see them trying to look casual as they watch what the city folk do, or sidling nonchalantly up to the new aerobics halls to sneak a look inside. They've woken up to modern city life and hope to acquire the latest mannerisms and fads to boost their images back in their villages.

Apart from having too many passengers on board our bus was also heavily loaded with commercial goods, a great teetering pile on the roof-rack. One extra-large bundle on the roof-rack had Cherent and I guessing about its contents though we never did discover what they were. It was a triangular shape and solid, with a long soft tubular piece attached to it. The triangle was wrapped in bright blue plastic and tied with narrow strips of goatskin which then lengthened and broadened to bind the long soft, wobbly tube. Cherent, who was always curious about what people were carrying and if it was legal or not (probably something to do with his job in the Wildlife Conservation Organisation) pondered for hours about the contents of this bundle and eventually asked the Eritrean man sitting opposite him, to whom he'd been explaining his work, what he thought it was. 'Forget about it,' he said, 'it's an endemic bundle.'

We creaked out of Assab and were immediately immersed in the desert. At first it was a grey, stony desert which gradually opened out into an expansive area of flat white sand with occasional sand-dunes. Every now and then a lone camel walked by with an apparently definite purpose about where it was going. How could it possibly know, I wondered, for everywhere looked the same. We passed the wreck of an Italian plane from the Second World War which the driver pointed out enthusiastically, though he wouldn't stop for me to take a photograph. His blood was up now after a couple of days of waiting, and he didn't want to be interrupted.

The driver had installed a 200-litre drum of water roped to one of the steel roof supports close to where Cherent and I sat. Within minutes of leaving the city passengers got up and jostled their way to the drum with their bowls and bottles for water. Nobody it seemed had actually considered filling their bottles before boarding the bus.

'I can't believe this,' I said. 'At this rate we'll never have enough water to last to Massawa.'

'Well, who knows,' said Cherent, not wanting to interfere with the driver's arrangements. The driver had made the trip many times before and presumably had matters in hand. But I found the reckless water consumption quite a worry, and clung tightly to our small jerrycan and water bottle. People in Africa rarely think about tomorrow, presumably because the future is so unpredictable. Just getting through today is preoccupation enough; tomorrow's bridges are crossed when one gets to them. With only one drum for everyone on board it seemed clear to most passengers that they had better grab now before the others had it all. The driver paid no attention.

The sandy scene engulfing us was deserted, but often littered with old wrecked tanks – hard evidence of the intensity and bitterness of the Eritrean-Ethiopian war of independence. Gradually the country became spotted with short thorny trees and as the sun rose and it began to get hot I knew we were in for an uncomfortable day. Last year in our own car we could stop and stretch and breathe whenever we wanted to, but the bus didn't offer this luxury. We rattled on across a lot more flat, dry, thorny scrub country. What looked like tumbleweed was caught up in many places on outcrops of little rocks, which were in great contrast to huge flat-topped mountains standing isolated on the horizon. As we passed near the small village of Wadi, about 160 kilometres from Assab, the landscape was dramatically dotted with two-metre high stone cairns marking the graves of people who had died in the war.

I was just thinking about how difficult the fighting must have been in this area, when a dreadful crash followed by a dragging noise came from underneath the bus. The driver stopped instantly to find that the fuel tank had broken off and was dragging along the stony ground with the contents spilling out of a hole made by a sharp rock.

The driver turned out to be a very skilful mechanic who was familiar with the desert and its problems, having been a driver in the Eritrean army. He was a cool, unflappable character and having seen the problem set his grease-monkey to siphoning the fuel out of the tank into an empty drum which he had stored on the roof-rack. Once the tank was empty he roped it back into place under the vehicle. Then, to everyone's surprise, he unscrewed a panel on the side of the bus to reveal another fuel tank. This was filled up from the drum.

During our stop we all took the chance to stretch our legs and on investigating the bus I discovered that we were carrying several drums of fuel. Obviously there was none to be had *en route*. It was very hot by now and I admired the driver who was oblivious to the heat as he worked on the fuel tank. The repair made we were on our way again, everyone chattering loudly about the incident. I began to feel a little apprehensive about the journey ahead of us, but I consoled myself with the thought that a trip without a few mishaps wouldn't be much fun.

By the time we arrived in Afambo at about two o'clock in the afternoon we were all ready for lunch. We had driven 240 kilometres and still had 180 kilometres to go to reach Thio, where the driver was planning to spend the night. Anyhow, he felt we were making reasonable time and could take at least an hour's break.

Looking around, I noticed that the village architecture was very attractive, much like that seen in Tigray, with little square buildings built of stone, no cement, with flat roofs. They were hardly visible against the rocky hills having been made from the same material.

Very few houses had any windows, just small doors, and they were perched on stone plinths about half a metre off the ground. Maybe this helped to keep sand out of the interiors, or more likely scorpions which are common in many deserts at night.

The houses were just scattered pell-mell with no village planning. A few of them, including the restaurant, were on the roadside. The restaurant was made from mats, a higgledy-piggledy construction which one would probably never have recognised as an eating house if it hadn't been for the Fanta and Coca-Cola signs tacked up on the outside. The menu offered a choice of spaghetti or goat *tibs* for lunch, but no 'Gordon Blue' (a common item on menus all over Ethiopia). Anyhow, we all agreed that we had a fine selection for a cafe 250 kilometres out in the desert.

I was told that most of the inhabitants of the village were families of people who had fought in the war of independence, and subsequently settled there. However, there were some Afar people living there too. The Afar territory stretches through Denkalia as far south as Gewane, and as far east as Dire Dawa in Ethiopia. They probably number 100,000 people and they are a proud race who can be both hostile and fierce. Some of them are still nomadic, living in fairly small, isolated family groups. In Ethiopia their dwellings are sometimes made from light grass mats woven from a coarse grass which grows on the banks of the Awash River. When the family wants to move on, the mats are rolled up and with all the other items are packed onto camels who take everything safely to the next encampment. In Dankalia I noticed Afar people living in many different types of dwelling depending on what materials were available to build with. Some of them had obviously settled in Afambo, bringing their goats with them and planned to take advantage of any developments in the area. I noticed a new government brick building on the outskirts of the town and I was told that it was a clinic and a school. How the people spent the day I could not imagine. The village was surrounded by the harshest, driest country with only a few camels and goats and no possibility of cultivation. Though there must have been a well, I didn't see it. I imagined the arrival of the bus once a week was quite an important event in their lives as it was a good income provider.

Having fed and watered well (though no one bothered to refill the drum) we climbed back into the bus and started off through a small mountain range to Thio, a five-hour drive away, so the driver said, as he didn't reckon on averaging more than 30 kilometres an hour. He hoped to reach Thio by nine that night. We hadn't driven for more than an hour when, with a loud grinding noise, the bus once again came to a halt. The right-hand front spring had collapsed. The afternoon sun was still blazing down and the heat, together with the after-effects of the well-spiced lunch, encouraged the passengers to help themselves to yet more water from the dregs of the drum. The repair of the spring took several hours and once night fell the driver used the headlights to carry on with the work. He well knew that this was not a good idea but was eager to keep to his schedule. Sure enough, the repair done and all of us back in our seats, the battery was too flat to start the engine. It took half an hour to organise a team of the strongest passengers to push-start the bus, but they managed. The charging system then turned out to be defective and even with the engine running there was no power to the headlights.

It was a cold, clear night with a half-moon lighting up the desert and so the driver decided to press on by the light of the moon. We set off at a snail's pace with discouraging noises coming from the botched-up spring at every little bump. Our misgivings were confirmed when after a couple of kilometres it gave way again. By this time the driver was completely exhausted and said he was going to get some sleep, and so should we. It was a strange sight, with little groups of people curled up on the sand around and under the bus in the middle of nowhere. One old man wandered around looking for a Somali girl he had taken a fancy to on the bus, so that he could curl up beside her. But when he did find her she gave him a mighty kick in the shin that sent him off into the night wailing like a hyena.

Early next morning the driver was back at work, assisted by some of the passengers who were eager to reach their destination. We had a government officer travelling with us to attend a meeting in Asmara. His department did not have the funds for him to fly. A better bus route would have been for him to go to Kombolcha in Ethiopia and then north again to Asmara. He said that before independence it was common for Assab people to travel that way, but now travel between the two independent countries was not as easy and so he was forced to take the Red Sea route. 'At this rate,' he said, 'the meeting will be over before I get there.'

As the sun rose the passengers warmed themselves like lizards and then busied themselves preparing breakfast tea on paraffin stoves to drink with bread or biscuits. Everyone washed and rinsed out their mouths, the drum now virtually empty. Most passengers were in high spirits, with not a care in the world. Several young women on board were evidently professional bar girls on their way to Asmara where, the grass being greener, they were going to make more money than they could in Assab. To pass the time they settled down to do each others' hair. It was like a family picnic. The hairdressing done they sang and danced and had more tea and washed again and the water in the drum was now little more than a splash. We hit the track again mid-morning.

The scenery changed dramatically as we drove through the tiny town of Belebuy. We had only travelled about 40 kilometres from Afambo, but now we were faced with huge, sultry, grey mountain ranges. The track was not built to climb across the bare mountains, but instead followed the valleys, crossing innumerable dry river beds. The air was still and stifling hot. We stopped in a small village called Ignoli for refreshments and I watched goats drinking at a water trough near a well. I plucked up courage and asked the driver if we shouldn't refill our water drum. But he said that it was now only about 80 kilometres to Thio and he didn't want to waste the time.

Ignoli was a series of igloo-like houses built from sticks. There were no rocks at all in the area, just dry thorn scrub which was cut and cleaned and then used as a building material. I wondered what the houses would be built of in a few years time when all the thorn trees had been demolished. Anyhow, I once again saw a government school and clinic in the distance, so there was obviously a plan to develop the village.

After Ignoli the journey continued through the mountains, with the interminable heat. People were tired by now and began to squabble over the small amount of water that was left in the drum. The stronger characters on the bus tried to stop the others from taking water, but these arguments were abruptly ended when the bus radiator boiled. Such water as remained was poured into the radiator. Now the major topic of conversation was water. How were they going to wash? How were they going to drink? Where would we find water? If we broke down again we might die of thirst. Then the spring collapsed again.

The party was over now and everyone was getting irritable. One woman with a child asked if they could drink from our water bottle. We had of course been expecting this. We had been strictly rationing our drinking and so were the only ones left with any water. All of a sudden we were the focus of everyone's attention. I felt like a wildebeest surrounded by lions. We gave the child a cup and told the woman that we'd soon be in Thio, so she would have to wait. Whilst the bus repair was being done the sound of a vehicle lightened the gloom and before long a truck drew up on the road behind us. Many of the passengers, including the government officer on his way to Asmara, begged for a lift. The truck was already packed full with people standing like sardines out in the burning sun, but the driver agreed to take some more on board. The government officer said he just wanted to reach Thio, so that he could phone Asmara and tell them that he was going to be late. He also hoped to get a lift with another vehicle out of Thio because his confidence in the bus ride was shattered. Cherent and I decided to stay with the bus. I didn't fancy playing sardines in the back of an open truck and preferred to take my chances with broken springs and boiling radiators.

Eventually the driver succeeded in botching the spring back into service again and we resumed our journey. Then a woman called to him from the back of the bus and he stopped. I looked around the seemingly empty desert to see why. At first I saw nothing and then I saw one small stick-igloo house built right beside the road. Just one structure, completely isolated. The woman collected her bags, climbed down and walked a few steps to the entrance of the igloo. A man appeared from inside and welcomed her. She had come home.

The spring held together and we arrived in Thio after dark. It was wonderful to hear the sea washing on the shore and to be out of the lonely desert. Although Thio is the biggest fishing village between Assab and Massawa it doesn't really cater for visitors. There are no hotels but a friendly bar provided us with food and then we all took to the sand again to stretch out our *gabis* and get some sleep. Of course my plan was to stretch out on the beach, but once again I was warned not to go near the place because it was the town toilet. As I settled down to sleep I reflected that we still had 305 kilometres to go and if the first 420 kilometres was anything to go by we could still be in for an eventful journey.

'In fact, it should only be a day's drive,' I said to Cherent. 'We know the road, don't we?'

'Most of it,' he laughed. 'We must look out for the place where we took the wrong turning last year.'

Thio was really just a single street lined with small, square houses, built of wooden planks and corrugated iron. The houses were painted, mostly green or red. Goats chewed on lemon skins or any other garbage which was swept along the street by quite a strong sea breeze. Outside the town large flocks of goats were visible through the haze of the blowing sand.

There was a garage in the town and the next morning we explored the place while the driver took the bus to the workshop. The inhabitants seemed to be predominantly Muslim and the women in their brightly-coloured clothes hid their faces from us and from the blowing sand.

By the middle of the afternoon the repairs were complete and we left town, headed for Galelo which was 157 kilometres to the west through a very soft sandy area with very few landmarks. Cherent and I tried hard to spot the place where we had taken the wrong turn the year before, but we couldn't find it. Besides, we were distracted by the bus radiator boiling again and we then discovered that the driver had not filled the water drum in Thio. We were stuck in the middle of the desert again, or so it seemed to us, but fortunately we were only a 20-minute walk from a well. The water was very brackish but it was good enough for the radiator and for those passengers who had already finished the water they had collected in Thio. By now everyone had begun to realise how important it was to have plenty of water with them, so those who were getting short accompanied the driver to the well. From then on we made good time until nightfall but as the repairs in Thio hadn't extended to the charging system we couldn't keep going because it was cloudy with no moonlight to drive by and the bus lights were too weak to show the way. We spent the night in a bleak spot, on the top of a stony rise where a bitter wind blew. I tried to shelter behind a wheel but it made a poor screen and an early morning start was most welcome.

The drive to Mersa Fatma was uneventful. We remembered Mersa Fatma by the four burnt-out Italian buildings that we had seen the year before. From Mersa Fatma the route along the pretty coastline was a wonderful relief from the desert of the previous days. The views were truly amazing. As far as the eye could see stretched a shimmering blue ocean with tiny white waves dancing in the wind. White sand partially covered with small purple boulders edged the ocean. In places an open area of sand hugged the coastline, to be turned into a field of solid purple boulders further inland which spread for miles and miles, with no beginning and no end. Further on the boulders were splashed with different colours: orange, yellow, grey and brown, as though an artist had been this way dabbing colours from his palette at random as he walked. Distant islands dotted the sparkling sea. In one place two camels raced ahead of us along the road, splashing through tidal puddles. Wide tidal salt pans, solid, flat and white, were crossed by a single-track rocky causeway, which the bus wobbled across. We reached Galelo without any further problems.

Galelo homes were different again from anything we had seen before. They were built from sticks, but they were square and not circular like the earlier igloo design. They had wooden doors painted in bright colours with various designs added in contrasting colours. There was a large, brick administrative centre at one end of the town and at the other end children and animals clustered around a well. I watched the children filling the water bags carried by their donkeys. The well was ten metres deep, and they had to drop a bucket down into the water on a rope and then drag it back up. It was very impressive to see how easily these young children managed the difficult task. They didn't tire, but got bored as the water bags were large and it must have taken at least an hour to fill one bag. When the children were bored, they sat and talked, seemingly exchanging news as if they hadn't seen each other for several days. Maybe they only took water from the well once a week. A few of them spoke a little English, but not enough to have a real conversation.

Galelo had a coastal customs post and so our stop there was very long. Everything had to be taken down off the top of the bus and each individual's luggage was opened and examined carefully. If we had any contraband on board it was either ignored or overlooked and finally we started our last lap, as far as I was concerned, down to the Buri Peninsula, and then up the steep, rocky escarpment to Irafayle, where we were to spend the night. As we passed by a particular rocky area I watched out for a small group of asses that I had seen on our previous trip sheltering from the hot sun in a shallow cave. At the time I had thought these animals were the endangered wild ass because they had very long ears, sleek coats and striped hocks, as though they were wearing football socks. I had made some enquiries about them in Addis but it seemed that they were either a cross between a wild ass and a donkey, or just an ordinary donkey, for they didn't have the correct markings on their shoulders to be the endangered wild ass. Besides, the animals I saw were very tame, and wild ass are very timid. I would like to have seen the animals again, but on this occasion they were nowhere in sight.

I have a particular affection for donkeys. Their intelligence impresses me and they seem to have a sense of humour. In Addis Ababa on a market day, the loaded animals hardly need to be accompanied by a driver for they have learnt where to take their loads. Once they have dropped their goods they can easily find their way home on their own, safely crossing busy streets with no fear of the traffic. One day I watched a group of donkeys carrying bales of straw to market and *en route* they passed another donkey group who were already dawdling home, having dropped their loads. One dawdler saw the bales of straw passing him by and with a gleam in his beady eye quickly rushed forwards and took a few large mouthfuls from one of the bales. 'Ah, meals on wheels,' he was probably thinking. His companions were happy to nibble at the roadside grass, but this one animal was challenging the other group and he was obviously enjoying it.

On another occasion when I was visiting Dima the Akobo River was in flood. I watched two donkeys coming back to Dima alone from a journey they had obviously made on the Maji side of the river carrying supplies to alluvial gold diggers. The animals saw the swirling, fast-flowing water of the flooding river and walked some way upstream from where you could see they usually crossed before they plunged into the raging water. I feared that they would drown, for only every now and then could I see their long ears sticking out above the surface of the water. Not a bit of it. They arrived at my side of the river and climbed out onto the bank at exactly the place opposite to where they would have normally plunged in. I was very impressed to see that they had learnt from other journeys when they were with their owner what to do under these dangerous circumstances.

When we had driven the hellish Buri escarpment the year before I had thought that we would never make it, because the rocky surface had been almost impossible to manage in the Toyota. The bus, being higher off the ground and with much bigger wheels, made less of a meal of it, although the hairpin bends had to be taken very carefully.

The exotic, sandy peninsular had filled us all with hope and we scaled the major part of the escarpment with ease. But as we rattled along a flatter part of the road before the final descent a spring U-bolt on the right-hand side of the bus sheered off and once again we were stopped in the desert. As we were only 20 kilometres from Irafayle some of the men decided they would walk to reach the town just after nightfall. The government officer, who was still with us as he hadn't managed to find a lift in Thio, was one of the people who decided to walk. He said he hoped to find a lift in Irafayle early next morning. I liked the idea of walking with them, but these men would be hard, fast walkers and I knew that I would not be able to keep up with them. So we settled down for another night on the roadside. This was a horrible rocky spot and I really was beginning to think we would never reach Massawa. The novelty of the journey was

71

over, and both Cherent and I were tired and hungry as I suppose everyone else on the bus was too.

Anyhow, I didn't sleep very well and at some point during the night I looked up to see what was rustling nearby. A magical scene was spread out before me. In the dim moonlight a camel train of 50 or more camels was passing by, just a few metres from where we all lay, with one or two Afar people walking with them. It was impossible to imagine how so many animals could make so little noise. I woke Cherent and the man sleeping next to him so they could see the sight. The man told us that it was a camel train going to the coast further east to collect contraband goods from boats coming in from the Yemen. I immediately thought of the village where we had spent the night a year before and peered through the night to see if there were any young girls riding on the camels. But it was too dark to see.

The driver fixed the breakdown early next morning and we arrived in Irafayle in time for breakfast. The men who had walked to the town the previous evening were just leaving for Faro in a pickup as we arrived. They told us a second pickup would be leaving the town soon. Cherent and I now decided to abandon our sinking ship and bagged front seats on the pickup which got us to Foro, 30 kilometres from Irafayle, in about an hour. Now there were about a dozen of us deserters in Foro and we spent the rest of the day looking for a car to take us the final 60 kilometres to Massawa. But there were no taxis, trucks or cars and by mid-afternoon we were still there when our bus limped in from Irafayle. The driver thought it was very funny that we hadn't found alternative transport, and welcomed us back on board. The bus was now in a very bad way. A second U-bolt had sheered off and the maximum speed for the final 50 kilometres was 20 kilometres per hour. We arrived at long last at nine in the evening. But the delicious thought of a hot bath and a big meal, not to mention a bottle or two of wine, was to remain just a thought, for when we reached the town we found all the hotels fully booked. It was perhaps fitting that we ended up spending the last night of our journey in a scruffy little hotel that was no more comfortable than our roadside camps, and a lot less clean.

The next morning we awoke early, but we didn't go to the bus station to meet our bus. We took a contract taxi to Asmara and caught the plane back to Addis. I was glad the journey was at last over and I looked forward to a few familiar creature comforts. But there were some special recollections that diminished the discomforts and frustrations. The large, cool bay of the Buri Peninsula and the ghostly camel train that passed in the night – I knew these would be indelible memories.

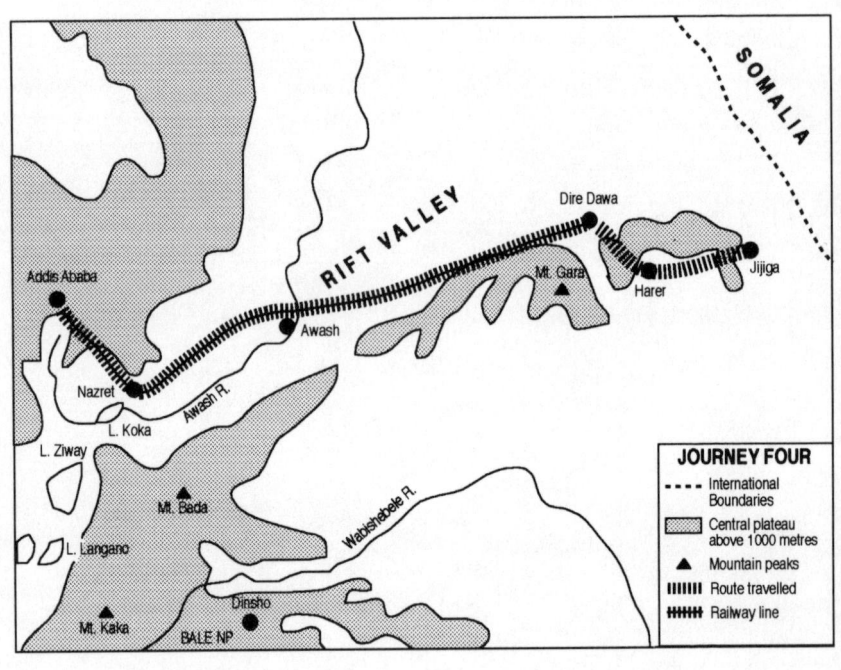

4

Anchen Calmeselish or Let It Be

I was feeling uncertain about travelling on the train to Dire Dawa. I had visited Dire Dawa and Harar several times before, twice in my own car, once by bus and once by plane. However, the train trip kept eluding me and every time I arranged to go something cropped up and I had to change my plans. Nevertheless I was determined to make the journey on Ethiopia's sole rail service that operated from Addis Ababa to Djibouti, via Dire Dawa. This railway, financed by the French government between 1897 and 1917, was to have opened up the interior to trade and development but though it still exists it never realised the dreams of its proponents and remains an outdated, little-used facility. I had always wanted to experience the train journey for myself having heard all sorts of stories about it.

The original steam engines have been replaced by diesel engines that are an integral unit with the first-class carriages. Before boarding we had to undergo a security search and as the officials were late I sat gazing out of the waiting room window. The outside of the first-class coach was well plastered with black diesel smut, so I resolved to sit as far away as I could from the engine. I could just see a toilet door immediately inside the door leading onto the platform. I was pleased to see we had a toilet on board because it was bound to get very hot once we descended into the Rift Valley which meant we would be drinking lots of beer and Coke.

At last we were given the green light to board. We hadn't been allocated particular compartments and on entering the first-class

75

carriage I saw why. The coach was not as I was used to, with compartments and bunk beds. It was simply arranged like a long-distance bus with rows of twin seats separated by an aisle. There were about 30 seats in all. Cherent and I settled into seats at the back, away from the diesel fumes and close to the toilet. A woman train attendant boarded the train just after we had chosen our place and coincidentally she turned out to be a neighbour of Cherent's from his suburb of Kasanjis. She was surprised at our seat choice and advised us to move forward. It was to be a long journey and she said that after a few hours the stench from the toilet would be unbearable and we shouldn't sit anywhere near it. It sounded like very good advice so we collected our bags and moved about halfway up the carriage, sitting next to a window. Windows were adjacent to every other row of seats.

'You must sit near a window,' she said, 'because the carriage gets very hot. Most of the passengers will not open their windows, because they are afraid of fresh air, so you have to be by your own window, then you can open and shut it as you want.'

The smell of diesel was very pungent throughout the carriage and it wasn't until we were on our way that I realised it had nothing to do with the engine. The whole carriage had been washed with diesel fuel. In Ethiopia paraffin or diesel is highly favoured for cleaning floors and the interiors of cars. Take your car for a service and it will be returned with all the vinyl upholstery and fittings soaked in paraffin that will keep you nauseated until it's due for the next service.

The almost universal phobia of open windows and fresh air that the attendant had reminded us of makes the practice of washing the insides of houses with paraffin a particularly inscrutable custom. I hoped that the diesel fumes might at least keep the toilet smell at bay for a few hours.

There was a small bar at the back of the carriage (near the toilet) selling beer, soft drinks and bread. Having heard the story about the toilet I now resolved to drink as little as possible, because from past experience I knew what a smelly toilet looked like inside. Anyhow, with seats in the middle of the coach, fortunately we were not overpowered by the smell of the toilet during the journey. Nevertheless I didn't dare use it and by the time we reached Harar, before even registering for a room, I had to make a rush for the hotel toilet.

If you travel in Ethiopia you soon learn that the design and use of toilets has been locked in a time warp. It seems that they are still experimenting with the first prototypes and finding it difficult to figure out where the designers goofed. The universally adopted ten-centimetre diameter hole in the floor that one encounters everywhere calls for a standard of marksmanship that mankind simply isn't possessed of. Centuries of practice hasn't improved their aim and one has the impression that everyone has simply given up hope of coming up with anything better.

Although the security people were late the train left Addis Ababa station on time, four o'clock in the afternoon. I felt very excited as we chugged out of the station. Cherent had let me sit by the window, and I pushed my head against the thick aluminium bars that crossed the window horizontally and peered out at the people who lived along the railway line. The bars were to stop thieves from climbing in the window at night when we were all asleep. From my point of view, they were a terrible nuisance because they were so close together it was impossible to put a camera between them.

We jolted through the city outskirts and I was amused to see that the people living along the railway line knew exactly which track the train would take, for they had set their market stalls up across all the other tracks. As we passed by we were within a few inches of stalls selling tomatoes, fruit, charcoal, soap, matches and other household necessities. It would have been a sorry scene if one day, without warning, the train used a different track.

As we pulled further and further away from Addis Ababa we picked up some speed and a cool breeze wafted into the carriage, taking away some of the diesel fumes. We were a mixed bunch. There was one teenage boy, and one family with a young child. Several elderly women were travelling alone. There was one other *ferenji* besides myself, travelling with a tour guide. The remaining passengers were either businessmen or railway staff returning to their posts after leave. Once the train really got going everyone found it amusing to watch each other bouncing up and down uncontrollably, sometimes to great heights, because the line, like the roads, is very rough. The laughter got us all talking to each other right away and the atmosphere was very friendly.

We stopped several times within the first couple of hours, at Dukem and then at Debre Zeit, Mojo and Nazereth. All these towns are on the main road from Addis to Dire Dawa and I had visited them many times before. It was interesting to see another side of them. None of the stations had a platform. Passengers wanting to board just stood between the railway lines flagging the train down, though I'm sure it would have stopped anyway. Apart from the first-class carriage we were pulling four third-class carriages that were absolutely packed with people sitting on each others' knees and almost hanging from the luggage racks. I admired the equanimity of these passengers who must have been extremely uncomfortable and hot. Frequently at stations I saw derelict carriages being used as homes and when night fell we passed one such with a family eating their evening meal by candlelight.

At every station hawkers offered a variety of peanuts, oranges, bananas, biscuits and so forth. Most people had brought food with them in their big *aglegel* (picnic baskets) and shortly after dark they sat around eating their *njera* and *fitfit*, (small pieces of *njera* soaked in sauce). The male travellers were more interested in *chat* than food. Nearly all of them had boarded the train with a bundle of green *chat* leaves, which when chewed have a mild stimulating effect.

It is common for men and women in Ethiopia to chew *chat*. A painter friend of mine told me that Muslim priests chew *chat* and the Orthodox Christian priests smoke and make tea with marijuana. I can well imagine that the priests need some kind of stimulant to keep them awake during their long hours of prayer every day. During special festivals like Easter the prayers, broadcast all day long over loudspeakers, can be very disturbing to one who is not a follower of the Orthodox religion. While the priests find a joint helps make prayers I tend to the view that it helps deal with their noise.

Some *chat* chewers add sugar to their mouthful to sweeten the bitter leaf. Hardened chewers disdain sugar. The leaf makes the

78

chewer very thirsty and large quantities of water or diluted Fanta or Coke are consumed. As Ethiopians simply drop their rubbish where they are our carriage was soon littered with stems and reject *chat* leaves, cigarette ends and so on.

Although I had expected the scenery to look completely different from the train than from a car, it actually looked much the same. At first the railway more or less followed the main road to the east out of Addis Ababa. About 20 kilometres out of the city it passed by the Akaki wetlands, a bird-watchers' paradise, which stretch for 12 kilometres to the south. Shortly after that, north of the small town of Dukem, about 25 kilometres from Addis, we could see the 3000-metre high Mount Yerer, an extinct volcano some 4 million years old. The train then chugged through a large area of farmland where the crops were already ripe and the farmers were out in the fields making hay. I think the railway line's position was higher than the main road and so I got a good impression of how extensive the farmlands surrounding Addis Ababa were. As evening approached and the light faded I was surprised to see a large number of farmers still at work. Unlike many rural people they appeared not to be frightened of the darkness with its marauding animals. Except for hyenas – that are everywhere in Ethiopia – there are hardly any large wild animals remaining in the countryside between Addis and Awash.

When we reached Awash at about seven o'clock in the evening it was already dark. Awash town by day is not a very attractive place and probably only exists because of the railway station. We made a long stop and many people got off the train to stretch their legs and buy food. I was happy to sit where I was and I mentioned to Cherent that I was glad we had crossed the causeway across the Matahara Lake (Lake Beseka) without incident. When you see the railway line by day where it crosses the rough lava on a precarious-looking causeway you wonder how the train ever reaches the other side. The lake itself is another bird-watchers' paradise and the scenery in the area is spectacular with Fentalle volcano looming out of the haze.

Matahara town came into being because of the large sugar plantations and fruit farms in the area. Awash National Park covers 837 square kilometres in this area, and visitors to the park

79

sometimes use the hotels in Awash town or Matahara as a base for visiting the park, where the accommodation is very expensive. Unfortunately as it was dark there would be no chance of any animal spotting from the train.

Shortly after we left Awash, the *chat* chewers, who by then had also drunk a couple of beers, took out sleeping mats, laid them on the rubbish-strewn carriage floor, and went to sleep. It was not easy to manoeuvre oneself to the bar across this obstacle course. However the sleepers appeared not to notice the odd finger being trodden on. Cherent and I tried to get our seats to recline but the ancient mechanisms were broken and so we spent the night sitting bolt upright.

The descent into the lowland around Awash had made the carriage hot and stuffy and just as Cherent's friend had warned, everyone had their windows closed. Mine was wide open, much to the disgust of an elderly lady sitting behind me. She complained bitterly to Cherent that she would get ill from the fresh air and that she was cold. I offered to lend her a sweater, and Cherent told her she was far more likely to get ill from the stale air of the closed carriage than from the outside air. She refused to use the sweater, and everyone else in the carriage smugly agreed with Cherent, though all of them kept their windows firmly closed.

I nodded off once we had safely crossed the rickety bridge high above the Awash River. We were both listening for it and were relieved to hear the train clatter across it without mishap. As I closed my eyes I imagined the wild animals prowling around in the dry acacia scrub.

During the night we changed seats so that Cherent could cool off by the window. I found Cherent's seat very hot and couldn't imagine how everyone else was so relaxed without any ventilation. I must have fallen asleep again and then later in the night when I heard the strain on the diesel engine as it started to climb I knew we would soon feel the cool air of the Arba Gugu mountains. I then slept for a long time.

I had not succeeded in taking many photographs before it grew dark and I'd told Cherent to wake me as soon as it was light so I could at least try to get a few more pictures. It was about four-thirty in the morning when he woke me. Everyone else was wide awake, combing hair and washing hands. I was astonished. Cherent told me that the ticket collector needed my ticket.

'Why?' I asked.

'Because we are just arriving at Dire Dawa,' he replied.

'Nonsense,' I retorted. 'We can't be. We have only been travelling for a few hours and we were told it would be a 16-hour journey. Besides, it isn't light yet and I haven't taken any photographs.' But sure enough Dire Dawa station was right there.

Overall, the journey had been a pleasant surprise. I had read, and people had confirmed what I read, that the train journey was a most unpleasant affair. It had been described as unbearably hot, very, very long, and with thieves all along the track who'd have all your possessions the moment you nodded off. Well, the journey had been warm in the Rift Valley, but by no means unbearably hot. It took exactly 12 hours 30 minutes – a good deal quicker than the 14-hour bus ride. No one on our train was robbed that I heard of. We were in the company of friendly, good-natured people with whom we shared a lot of laughs. It was altogether a pleasant, interesting experience I wouldn't have missed for anything, and vastly to be preferred to the bus trip.

When we got off the train in Dire Dawa the station seemed to be littered with brightly-coloured cloths like a field of variegated flowers. Looking closer I saw that the cloths were wrapped round sleeping Muslim women waiting to board the train for Djibouti. They must have spent a sticky night lying out in the station car park, for Dire Dawa is a sultry place.

The city is divided in two by a *wadi* (river bed) that only flows after rain. The old city south of the *wadi* is a maze of twisting streets lined with Arab-style houses. There is also a busy covered market in this area. The newer part of the city is not a very lively place except during the biannual pilgrimage to the hilltop church of Saint Gabriel in Kalubi, 20 kilometres away. Over 100,000 Christian Ethiopians from all over the country make the pilgrimage to Saint Gabriel, flooding the hotels and briefly turning Dire Dawa into a busy, crowded town.

When we arrived the town was very quiet, the silence broken only by the piercing cries of the taxi drivers shouting their taxi

81

routes to prospective passengers. We headed for a minibus going to Harar and climbed in. We were going to spend a few days in the 1000-year-old city of Harar, the fourth holiest place in Islam after Mecca, Medina and Jerusalem.

The minibus driver turned out to be demented, careening and squealing round the escarpment hairpins at a terrifying speed mostly on the wrong side of the road. Fortunately it was uphill or I could not have believed we would make it.

We hadn't been travelling more than ten minutes when the passengers in the rear seats of the car told him to stop and then started a violent argument. I briefly hoped they were remonstrating about his driving style but of course that was too much to hope for. Ethiopians never seem to object to the things that disturb *ferenji*, such as the toilets or maniacal drivers, or anything which I suppose is attributed to God's will. What was upsetting the passengers was the fare. The driver was demanding six birr, but the passengers reckoned that the correct fare was five birr. There was a very heated exchange at the end of which the driver told the passengers to disembark and get another taxi. Of course they were not prepared to do this and then accused him of putting the fare up because a *ferenji* was on board. I didn't want to sit on the road all day while they quarrelled so I told the driver that I would pay six birr if he insisted but that the other passengers should not be surcharged because of me. He retorted angrily that what he charged them was nothing to do with my presence. It was because, he said, that it was before seven in the morning, at which time of day a premium was payable. I have no idea how the thing was resolved but not long after this we resumed our journey.

Harar is famous as a mediaeval walled city. Although the city has long since spilled outside the confines of the perimeter wall, sections of the original structure still stand at many places. The older part of town preserves its ancient look with narrow, labyrinthine streets and flat-roofed houses. The main inhabitants are the Harari, called the Aderi by the neighbouring Oromo.

These people are well known for their stylish houses reminiscent of Arab coastal architecture. These are typically two-storey stone buildings with thick walls and flat roofs. Inside, the

82

main room has raised platforms at various levels to determine the rank and status of guests and household members. Thick, brightly coloured carpets hug the platforms, and the walls are elaborately decorated with bowls, dishes and basketry that are taken down and used when the need arises. Off to the left of the main room there is usually another room with a small latticed window opening onto the main room. This little room is a nuptial suite for a bride of the house and her husband after they are married. They stay in it for a week after the marriage ceremony. Nobody may enter and anything they want is passed through the window. This custom must certainly test the durability of any marriage and to come through it successfully would give newly-weds considerable confidence in the future.

The Harari-style honeymoon by confinement contrasts strongly with the more laid-back Oromo tradition. One evening we were driving back to Dinsho from Gobe in the Bale mountain area. A setting sun lit up the cloudy evening. The farmers had left the land and all was quiet. Suddenly, just in front of the car, a donkey stepped out into the road. A man and a woman were on the animal's back. They both had on white traditional dress, and the girl's *netala* fell over her face. The donkey walked slowly and serenely across the road as if it was carrying Mary and Joseph. They were followed by three cattle that had been sprinkled with short, dry blades of grass. These two people with their animals trotting across the wide, empty plain seemed in that moment so free.

'Who are these people?,' I said to Cherent as I gazed at the tranquil scene.

'They are newly-weds coming from their wedding and now going to the husband's house,' he replied. 'Tomorrow they will go back to their farming.'

Harar, with its 95 mosques, is the spiritual heart of Ethiopia's Muslim community. The country's population is 40 per cent Muslim, 40 per cent Christian and 20 per cent other denominations or pagan. Although the city dates back to the ninth century Harar became well known in the sixteenth century when, for 40 years the Muslim leader Ahmed Gragn used it as a base to fight the Ethiopian Christians. In the mid-sixteenth century, Gragn's nephew Nur Ibn al-Wazir built a five-metre wall around the city to protect it from the Oromo who had taken advantage of the Muslim-Christian war to invade large areas of southern Ethiopia, as far west as Jima.

During the next two centuries Harar remained an important Muslim centre with passage past the wall forbidden to all infidels. The city became well known to Europe when Sir Richard Burton, the nineteenth-century explorer, succeeded in passing through the wall disguised as an Arab. Once inside the holy city he lost his nerve and revealed himself to the Emir, who kept him prisoner for ten days, before releasing him to escape and disappear.

Thereafter Harar lost its power and influence. In 1865 it was captured by the Egyptians who held it until 1875 when Menelik, prince of Shoa, captured it. He put a Christian governor in place, Ras Mekonnen, the father of Haile Selassie. The French poet, Arthur Rimbaud, came to Harar in 1880 and lived there as a trader until his death in 1891.

There are three or four good tourist guides in Harar. I am speaking of the licensed ones, because, of course there are numerous small boys and men of every age and description who would like to show you around the city. Unofficial guides tend to give themselves away by approaching you and saying, 'Hello, I think I know you', when of course you have never laid eyes on them before.

When we first arrived in Harar we couldn't find a guide office and we learnt later that in fact there wasn't one. The way to contact a guide, we were told, was to telephone them at a bar in the centre of the city. Then if someone was available you could start the day with a hefty drink before your trudge around the city. We found it was easy to get this bar telephone number from either of the two major Harar hotels, the Ras and the Belainah. In fact, there is a third hotel a little way out of town, the Tana. The only thing I had against the Tana, which supplied excellent raw meat for those who liked to eat this traditional dish, was that the butchery was slap beside the dining room. The stench from the butchery quite put me off eating anything at all so although the bedrooms in the hotel were fine I've crossed the place off my list of preferred places to stay.

Generally, small Ethiopian hotels are friendly and do their best to make every individual as comfortable as possible and offer a variety of foods. This is not always so with the more sophisticated large hotels in the north of Ethiopia, where cavalier staff tend to be dismissive of individuals in favour of pandering to large group tours. Prepaid room reservations for individuals are as secure as a pile of feathers and you may well find yourself being dished up with the scraps from yesterday's group in the dining room, or their second-hand bed sheets on your bed.

One of these hotels has a real scam going. I arrived there on a later journey with a confirmed prepaid (in foreign currency) booking voucher. When the receptionist saw it he fumbled around with it for a bit and then looked at me saying that I owed him 12 birr. 'Why', I asked him. 'How can that be when everything was confirmed by your head office?'

'Well', he said, 'the exchange rate has changed since you made the booking and you are liable for the difference.'

'Ah – that means if the rate changes the other way tomorrow *you* will pay *me* the difference,' I said.

'Oh no, I can't do that,' he said, to which I replied then neither could I. After all, it sounded like a great little scam and I wanted to play too. I asked him if he was planning to open his own hotel soon – at 12 birr a person and an average of 30 guests a day he should be salting away 10,800 birr a month. Not bad for a hotel clerk. But by this time he'd remembered something else to do and wasn't listening.

Our Harar guide, Abdul Ahmed, told us that the old city within the wall was still predominantly Muslim and the Christian community was mainly located in the newer part of town outside the wall. Some of the old wall still existed but a large section had been rebuilt by the Italians. It was not difficult to see which was old wall and which was new, as the newer sections were built with a much brighter red stone.

The gate through which Burton entered the city was still there though it had been closed off and there was a shop operating in front of it, and a store behind it. We went to visit the tomb of Gragn's nephew, Emir Nur, who was responsible for building the wall. We also visited the tomb of Abadir, who I understand was a man who came from Saudi Arabia to Harar probably in the ninth century to teach Islam. On arriving at this tomb we found a relative of the dead man in attendance, a sheikh, who for a few birr offered to solve any problems that we might have. He appeared to be a very powerful healer because there was a queue of people waiting for his cures and these folk were not all Muslims: some were Christian Orthodox and some were other denominations. I couldn't think of any immediate problems so we walked into the garden behind the tomb. It was brim-full with ancient gravestones where all Abadir's relatives were buried. Local people visited this place daily and left burning incense at the graves, creating a garden of heavenly perfumes. Every now and then in the Harar wall there are drain holes, said by some to be used nightly by marauding hyenas. However, we were told it was not a good place to see these animals and we were persuaded to go to watch the hyena man feeding hyenas once night fell. This hyena feeding has been a feature of Harar for decades during which time the original hyena man has died and his offspring have taken over the job.

I enjoyed the show very much. It was a very black night and our car lights illuminated a slim man with a Rasta hairstyle. He was dressed in a sarong and sat out in an open place beside a bag of offal. He called out into the night, three or four times, something that I didn't understand. Then, in the car lights, pairs of eyes started to appear, and then whole animals walked into the amphitheatre and nervously approached the man. At first he threw pieces of food to them, but as they became more bold he held bones at arm's length and they came right up to him and took the food from his hand. Since that time I have heard that this hyena man is out of favour and there is a new show for tourists. The new hyena man holds bones in his mouth and the animals take them from there. This sounds a bit too risky to me, for an animal with a big mouth will surely take the man's head off one day. In the meantime there is some discussion about whether these hyenas should be encouraged at all for recently the Harar municipality wrote to the Ethiopian Wildlife Conservation Organisation in Addis Ababa, requesting that an officer go to Harar and shoot as many hyenas as possible, because they were getting out of hand.

Harar is not only busy at night, but it also bustles by day with a Muslim and a Christian market. Around midday life slows down when shopkeepers move to the backs of their shops and collapse into a *chat*-chewing stupor.

The countryside around Harar is one of the major *chat* growing areas in Ethiopia and large amounts of the plant are exported to Arabia. Although *chat* is legal, marijuana is not, though it has no more of an adverse effect on the taker than *chat*. *Chat* can drive people crazy.

One afternoon when the city was reasonably quiet I decided to take a walk from the hotel to the museum. The main street was not very crowded and I dawdled along looking in the shop windows for unusual jewellery. Once back on the pavement, I noticed a skinny, old woman walking straight towards me. She seemed to be in another world and her eyes were blazing red. I didn't move to the left or the right as I expected her to do that. Often nobody takes the initiative to change direction, and then at the last moment you are caught in a kind of dance, hop to the right, hop to the left, hop to the right, hop to the left, until one person takes the initiative to go to the left whilst the other person goes right, allowing a way through. Anyhow the old lady and I didn't reach the dancing stage for when she was a few metres from me she suddenly broke into a run and came straight for me. Before I had time to think she had crashed into me, knocking us both flying. I fell down on the pavement. She ran on as if nothing had happened. The other pedestrians were quite embarrassed and as they helped me up they told me that she had had too much *chat*. Did I want them to catch her so that she could pay me some compensation? I laughed. 'Compensation?' I said. 'For a grazed knee? How would we ever decide the price, and where would she get the money from, for a start?'

It reminded me of a week earlier when I had been sitting in a coffee shop in Addis Ababa. At the next table to me were three Tigray businessmen, a young street boy and his sister. Cherent told me that the three men were negotiating compensation with the young boy and his sister because earlier in the day they had accidentally knocked the young boy down with their Mercedes car. The police had taken a statement and then asked the businessmen to take the boy to the hospital to see if he had any serious injuries. If not, then they should negotiate compensation with the boy. The hospital said the boy had a badly bruised leg and prescribed painkillers. At the coffee shop table a statement was being written out for the boy to sign saying that he had negotiated with the men and that he had received a cash payment as compensation. Once he had completed the deal, he hobbled off, supported by his sister. He obviously had a very sore leg.

'Well,' I said to Cherent. 'How much did they give him, those rich businessmen?'

'You won't believe it,' he said. So I thought they must have been very generous. But I was wrong. 'Fifteen birr,' said Cherent. 'And now they are drawing up an account of what the incident has cost them.' It turned out that they were grumbling about the fact that they had had to spend, much against their will, a total of 48 birr to settle an accident which was caused by them.

Harar is one place in Ethiopia where it is possible to be very rich one day and poor the next. This is because a large number of people there live off black-market trading. Harar's proximity to the border with the Somali Republic attracts a lot of people who want to get rich quick. Jijiga, 109 kilometres east of Harar, is also known for its interesting market that is well stocked with contraband goods. This lifestyle is a dicey business and even though many people do succeed, others lose everything they have. It's a gamble and like all gambles there are winners and losers. Once, when we were driving to Jijiga to visit one of Cherent's relatives, we offered to give one of our hotel companions a lift. He asked us to drop him on the road about 15 kilometres out of Harar, in the bush, where there were no villages or farms. I was very curious about what he was going to do out there, so I asked him why he wanted to be dropped in such a God-forsaken place. He told us that he was meeting a truck there and some women who were his 'carriers'.

'Carriers,' I said. This wasn't making any sense to me at all. 'What do they carry? Gum leaves, fuel wood?'

'No,' he said, 'nail scissors.'

Nail scissors. It sounded like a post-modern artistic performance work. I could just imagine a group of women pushing their

In the seemingly empty desert I saw one small stick-igloo house built right beside the track. A woman jumped down from the bus. She had come home.

The crippled bus.

Thio.

Nechisar National Park. Lake Abaya has a reddish brown tinge.

Lake Chamo has clear icy blue water.

I was much too tired to start cooking so Shifferaw and Cherent said they would make the evening meal.

Grass plain in Omo National Park.

Lesser kudu in Mago National Park.

Waterbuck in
Mago National Park.

Lioness in Omo National Park.

Karo women.

Mursi woman.

The Harar wall.

Chat sellers.
Harar is one of the
major *chat* growing
areas in Ethiopia.

The gate through which Sir Richard Burton entered Harar in the nineteenth century is now closed off and a shop operates in front of it.

One of Harar's ninety-five mosques.

way through the scrub, each balancing a pair of nail scissors on their head – a surreal dance ceremony. He spoilt that scene by explaining to me that a truck was going to offload for him something like 50 cartons of nail scissors that he had bought on the black market in Hartshic. His carriers would pick them up from this spot and walk to Harar with them through the bush in order to avoid the customs post. He went on to explain that this was the beginning of a new venture for him. He had worked the black market for many years and five months earlier he had invested everything he'd earned on a load of something, I can't remember what, and the customs had caught him and taken everything. So he was starting out again from scratch.

'Why don't you give up and get a proper job?' I asked.

'Impossible, it's my way of life,' he grinned.

This wasn't my only contact with smugglers. On the bus journey back from Harar, Cherent and I were amazed to find that about 50 per cent of the people on the bus were black marketeers. Once the bus had left Harar on its way to Addis Ababa, and we had settled back into our seats, a young woman walked up and down the bus aisle with a large sack of goods that she started to distribute to all the passengers – sunglasses, shoes, shirts, dresses, jackets, handbags, calculators and trousers. I was asked to put on some sunglasses and a shirt. I didn't really know what was going on. I declined but sat and watched others don all manner of items. It was like a fancy dress party. The man behind me put on a pair of new jeans. This turned out to be the wrong thing to do because the owner of the jeans arrived at her destination before the wearer and an argument started up because he didn't want to take the jeans off in public when she wanted to leave the bus. Another woman put on five dresses. She was foiled at one of the customs checks and the customs officer had her strip them off one after the other.

There are at least four customs checks on the Harar-Addis road, and at one point we were at the end of a queue of ten buses waiting to be searched. Searching took place after all the passengers had left the bus. This didn't seem to make any sense to me because the searching officers must have known that most of the contraband goods left the bus with the passengers. Everyone alighted wearing sunglasses, new jeans and jackets, carrying adding machines and computers. It was all so obvious, though no doubt it wasn't worth the candle trying to prove that every pair of sunglasses was not the wearer's property. Nevertheless contraband can still sometimes be found on board and one officer had the driver undoing all the panels of our bus. Bingo! He found a great stash of new clothing worth 5000 birr that was confiscated on the spot leaving the owner in tears. It was not his lucky day. All confiscated goods are auctioned and the proceeds go into the government coffers, so I am told.

At the first customs post I noticed a ton of clothes piled outside, not protected from sun or rain. I learnt that this was second-hand clothing that had been confiscated from a truck some weeks earlier. I couldn't believe how unconcerned the customs officials were about this huge pile of good clothing. In Europe people go to such trouble to carefully wash and iron their used clothing before taking it to organisations like Oxfam to send overseas to homeless, poor people. And here on the Addis-Harar main road was a pile of those same clothes just wasting. At that very time Ethiopia was making an appeal abroad for help for all their flood victims.

The other event that surprised me a little on the bus was that the Christian Orthodox church made a collection. Ethiopian bus stations are always full of beggars and some beggars try to collect on board, but I've never seen the church on board before, cornering passengers and making it awkward for them not to donate. One young man on the bus took the whole matter quite in his stride for he needed some change. As the priest approached him, he reached out and, much to the priest's horror, took the whole collection. He then counted it and replaced it with the equivalent notes.

Beggars in Ethiopia come not only in every size and shape but each has his own begging style. Many genuine poor men, women and children probably never make the streets to beg because they are too ill or too hungry to move from where they lie, and I'm sure hundreds of them die alone and unremembered. However, many homeless people have built themselves beds out of rocks to raise themselves above the pavements to keep dry.

You can see little groups of these elevated beds, frequently by traffic lights, so that these rockery rats do not have to walk too far to find an income. In the rain, these people lie in their rockeries in plastic bags with their faithful hounds beside them.

When Ethiopia changed its currency one of these beggars went to the bank to change his takings which he had stored in his cloak of many pieces for some years. The beggar was astonished to hear from bank officials that he had collected 15,000 birr from his begging. He was also amazed to be told that they would open an account for him because it wasn't safe for him to carry that amount of money around. He wasn't keen but they took all his money away and put it in the bank for him.

Beggars that one sees all too often are the poseurs, the commercial beggars. Some of these people have jobs and beg for extra income. They usually try to catch foreigners at traffic lights, and a high proportion of them are women who carry other peoples' children as a ploy to make you feel sorry for them. They must be other peoples' children because it is not physically possible to produce the number of small children that some of them have clinging to their skirts.

Then, of course, there are the church beggars, the priests. I find it most offensive to be asked by a priest to give money. In my understanding of religion the priest should be handing out money to the poor, not collecting it. Then there is the government facilitator as a beggar. This is stretching a point slightly, but in Ethiopia there are plenty of government people whose job it is to help foreigners, but they absolutely refuse to do anything without begging for money. At road junctions in Addis one also comes across the musical beggar, who thinks that if he plays you a few notes on a pipe you will reward him handsomely. If you ask him to play a few extra notes he protests that he doesn't have the time because he has to go to the next car.

My biggest surprise has been to find group begging, when a whole pack of young men approach your car asking for money. I'm sure some people are intimidated by a bunch of begging ruffians and that's why this sort of begging is becoming increasingly popular. Recently in Addis Ababa two young men hit on a good ruse. They found some grass which they stuffed into a shirt and trousers. They installed their fake body on the pavement beside them with a *gabi* wrapped around it. They told passers-by that the man had come to town from the countryside and died. Because he had no relations in town they were collecting money to bury him. They were doing very well until a policeman became suspicious and snatched away the *gabi* from the 'body'.

The street kids alternate between hawking and begging depending on what sort of mark they size you up as. They operate with an extremely limited English vocabulary that they use without any inflexion so that the words are simply strung together. This produces some memorable epithets. Two common ones that at first you take for an address are 'Father Banana' and 'Mister Chewing Gum'. It takes a moment or two to realise you are actually being offered something for sale rather than being greeted. The same child, seeing you aren't buying, will then fall back on the universal pleas of 'stommak zero', 'you, money', or 'I am a crimple boy'.

In Harar by contrast there are not many beggars. People there generally seem to be quite well off with a sharp eye for the genuine article. One day when I was walking in the market with Cherent, wearing my favourite gold-plated earrings, a woman called over to Cherent, 'Why isn't the *ferenji* wearing real gold?'

On my last visit to Harar, I awoke one morning to find the city completely silent, no people calling and no dogs barking. It must have been about five o'clock and there was not a sound to be heard. I climbed out of bed and went to stand on the little veranda outside my room. Harar was nowhere to be seen. It was veiled in a very thick mist. It was like a ghost town, muffled and still. Suddenly the most beautiful song burst through this muffled silence. It was as if it was being played for all the Harar inhabitants on a loudspeaker. It seemed to be a love song and it was wafting its way into everyone's early morning. It was so magical. It summed up the very special, romantic character of this ancient city. The song stopped, the mist lifted and the day began. I had no idea where the music had come from but I knew that I hadn't wanted those moments to end, because only occasionally in one's life does something like that happen when one's spirit seems to be lifted and life becomes worthwhile.

I wanted to know where the song had come from and who was the singer. That evening when I was sitting on my veranda and people were packing up their stalls for the night just below me, suddenly there was a wail and a chant started up in the market place. I saw a small boy with something tucked under his arm rush past on the street below my veranda. A huge crowd pursued him chanting loudly as they went. He had obviously stolen something and I feared for his life if they managed to catch him. I was worrying about him. But then I heard the song again. It was far away in the distance and it was coming closer by the minute, and then it was in the street right beside the hotel. The daily bus from Jijiga had made its return journey. It had left the Harar bus station at five in the morning and now it was back. The bus loudspeaker was still playing this beautiful song. I later learned that it was Ethiopia's well-known singer Ephraim Tameru singing 'Anchen Calmeselish', translated in English as 'Let it Be'.

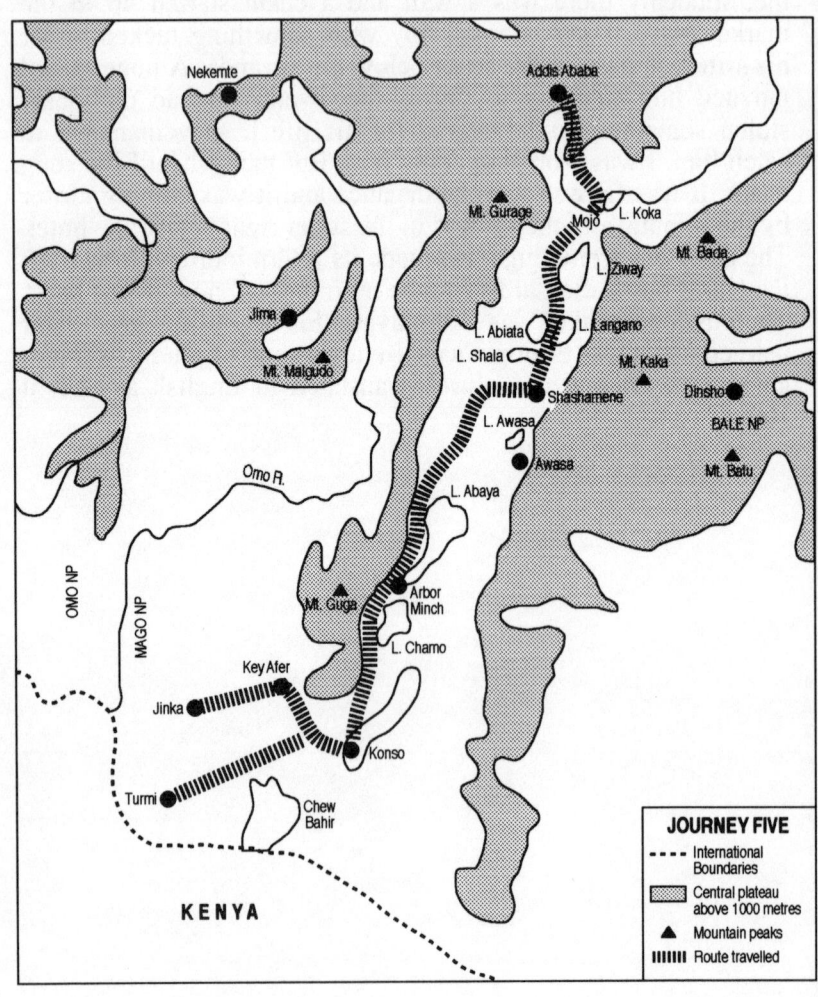

94

5

Stupid Animal

Geoffrey Harmsworth, in his *Abyssinian Adventure* of 1935 says 'Addis Ababa was built less than fifty years ago, and today, in spite of the efforts of Haile Selassie, it is little more than an untidy conglomeration of stone and mud huts, roofed with thatch or corrugated iron.'

John Gunther in his 1955 book, *Inside Africa*, says 'Addis Ababa looks as if it had been dropped piecemeal from an aeroplane carrying rubbish.'

In *The Heart of Ethiopia* 1972 Duncan Forbes says 'The general impression that I received in those few moments between skimming over the Entoto Hills and landing at Bole on the other side of the city was of a hill station like the ones I had seen in India, swollen to extraordinary proportions.'

Nowadays, Addis is all of this and more. Not only are there more slum houses but there are many more modern buildings and skyscrapers that have been and are still being built by rich Ethiopian businessmen as well as by foreign investors and organisations. To complement this modern development, there is an increasing number of middle-class Ethiopians and so there are more cars, buses and taxis.

There are also many more animals in the streets – sheep, cattle and donkeys. The donkeys carry farm products to the market and the sheep and cattle are for sale on the hoof, especially at festival times. There is also more rubbish in the city. Although the pavements are littered with piles of building materials and all manner of refuse and debris, often in such quantities as to force the

95

pedestrian off them, the roads for some curious reason are routinely swept clean. This strange chore is performed by headless women – or so at any rate they appear at first sight. Sweeping busy roads is a dusty not to say daredevil occupation and the practitioners dress for the job: full-length, grey dresses with high collars and long sleeves are topped with bandannas wound round the face to eye level. The ensemble is crowned by wide-brimmed straw hats whose size is such that instead of fitting *on* the head they fit *over* it. It's only when the wearer glances up from her work that you can reassure yourself that it is not, in fact, a headless person you are watching.

'Only the centre really looks like a town. The rest is a widely scattered settlement, the village huts and European-type houses, and various habitations of intermediate status, being all hidden away in great groves of Australian gum-trees.' Although David Buxton wrote this in 1949 in his *Travels in Ethiopia*, and in spite of the growth of the city since that time, his observation still accurately describes the city. It is still surrounded by Australian gum-trees that were brought to Ethiopia by Menelik II at the beginning of the twentieth century. The reason is that blue gums are fast-growing and hardy and therefore a better source of fuelwood and building materials than the slower-growing native trees that have all but disappeared.

Addis is a friendly city and compared to many African capitals it has very little violent crime. Even during large festivals like Meskel (the alleged finding of Christ's cross by Queen Elleni) and Timket (Ethiopian Epiphany, when Jesus was baptised in the river Jordan by his disciple John) the crowds are well behaved. I can bear witness to that because I have attended both these ceremonies for two years in a row.

In particular I was very impressed by the discipline at the Timket ceremony in 1996 when I walked with the procession. Emotions were running high, as always during a religious celebration. Cherent and I decided to go and wait at St Mariam church in Amist Kilo on Timket Eve. Amist Kilo means Five Kilometre. In Addis there is Arat (Four) Kilo, and Sidist (Six)Kilo too, so named because they are that many kilometres from one of the banks in the centre of town. On Timket Eve every Christian

Orthodox church in Ethiopia will take its *tabot* (copy of the ten commandments) and carry it in procession to a traditional pool nearby, where a service is held the following day.

Amist Kilo was an excellent vantage point, for there we would be able to see the bishop leaving St Mariam church to meet up with processions from three other churches before making their way to Jalmeda where they would all spend the night together nearby the traditional pool, in readiness for the next day's ceremony.

Jalmeda is a park on the outskirts of Addis where a large pool has been built for the occasion. The word Jalmeda derives from Janhoye Meda, meaning Haile Selassie's (Janhoye, a name given to Haile Selassie) field (*meda*). The large open field was so named because it was the first place an aeroplane landed in Addis Ababa. During the Dergue regime Mengistu changed the name to Jalmeda.

It was an eerie evening. In the far distance we could hear the pounding of drums accompanied by chanting. As this grew nearer, we saw the processions from the downtown churches making their way towards us, displaying all the wealth of the church with a multitude of priests clothed in brocade gowns carrying velvet and gilt umbrellas. Suddenly the bishop's procession burst out of St Mariam church and made its way out onto the street to meet up with the oncoming groups. The road was lined on both sides by scores of people, who clapped and wailed, but didn't move until the processions had passed. Thereupon they fell in line to walk behind the church procession. There was no pushing or unruly behaviour and there was no one there to line them up. It was astounding to see thousands of people take to the street so peacefully and in such an orderly fashion.

Recently, travelling back from Nairobi, my plane was delayed and I started talking to two young Ethiopian men who had been to a workshop in Kenya. I asked them how they, in modern times, saw the Orthodox church. What influence did it have in Ethiopia. They hesitated for a while, then one said he was a Roman Catholic so he didn't want to comment. The other one, however, said that he saw it as a unifier. It was an important part

97

of Ethiopian life that many of the uneducated people depended on. I reminded him about the religious fracas that took place recently in Arba Minch in southern Ethiopia, and asked him if the time for religious unification wasn't over. Nowadays people felt free to support other denominations. What happened in Arba Minch clearly showed that the Orthodox church was anything but a unifier. There is a strong Protestant following in that town. These Protestants asked the zone officials if they could hold a religious meeting in a field where for the past 33 years the Orthodox church has celebrated Timket. Much to the horror of the Orthodox followers, the administrator, a Protestant himself, agreed. The morning of the meeting arrived and they proceeded to the field only to find that the Orthodox faction had staked out the place. The police were summoned and started shooting over the heads of the combatants. They soon emptied all the clips for their AK 47s whereupon they were routed by the Christians. There followed a two- or three-day battle that brought the town to a complete standstill. A few people died, many were wounded and scores were jailed. The administrator remembered an urgent appointment in another town and decamped. Eventually the army was called in and law and order restored.

Orthodox followers never really get a good deal. At every celebration it is the people who end up giving to the church. One of the most common gifts for an Orthodox churchgoer to give the church is a brocade umbrella, used daily by the priests to protect them from the sunshine. However, all the churches already have so many umbrellas that they have set up church shops to sell off all the surplus. Every time there's a ceremony, people go to the church shop to buy an umbrella, that in turn is given to the priests, who already have too many and put it back in the shop to be bought again. So one single umbrella can become a handsome source of income for the church and a substantial loss of income for the poor parishioner, who may easily buy the same umbrella several times over.

At major celebrations, like Timket, ironically it is only the churchmen and the foreigners who get to see any more of the ceremony than the procession up the main street to the traditional pool. The following day the masses are kept well at bay by the police, with leather whips, and they only manage to hear the bishop and his cronies during prayers by loudspeaker. There is no way that they can see him as he blesses the water in the pool. Foreigners, on the other hand, who are not even Orthodox followers, are allowed to stand within a few metres of the bishop where they can absorb the glory of the ceremony and take photographs. Once the water has been blessed the church officials have it sprinkled directly on their heads, but for the common people a gigantic rotating water sprinkler is suddenly turned on in the park and everyone is simply showered *en masse* like a huge flower garden.

In Ethiopia Christian Orthodox ceremonies are very visible and well known to all. Much less well known is the biannual Muslim pilgrimage to the tomb of Sheikh Hussein in the southeast of the country. Sheikh Hussein is described by Graham Hancock in *African Ark* as 'possibly the first Islamic missionary ever to leave the relative safety of the coast and to penetrate deep into the heart of Ethiopia'. He spent his life preaching in the then inaccessible Bale province where he died in the middle of the fifteenth century and was canonised as a Sufi saint. Since that time his tomb has been visited by Muslim pilgrims twice a year. Pilgrims can be seen on the road all over Ethiopia headed to the sheikh's tomb several months before the ceremony. Many of these pilgrims spend their lives walking or travelling by donkey to the tomb and then, having nothing else to do, travel on to the south through the foothills of the Bale mountains to another shrine devoted to another Muslim saint. This man, Sof Omar, had also journeyed from the Somali coast into the hinterland where he discovered the entrance to a huge cave system. He decided to live in these caves and conduct his mission from them. Priests continue to attend the holy galleries of the Sof Omar Caves and pilgrims trek there from Sheikh Hussein (now a small town where the tomb lies) to pay their respects.

I had visited the Bale area in mid-1996 when one of the Bale Mountain National Park staff was seconded to the Southern Parks Project in Addis Ababa. There was no office transport available to collect his baggage from Bale and bring it to Addis so Cherent and I volunteered to go to the park headquarters to collect his stuff. It was a tedious trip for many reasons. First of all, I decided to take the road from Nazreth to Asela, Dodola, and Dinsho, instead of going down the asphalt to Shashamene and then travelling east to Dinsho. Addis to Asela was also an asphalt road, but from Asela to Dodola the road was very, very rough and every few kilometres something would fall off the old Toyota obliging us to stop and make repairs.

Second, this route reminded one strongly of the environmental damage taking place in the area. Asela is the capital of the Arsi district, that, in times gone by, used to boast a large number of wild animals. I saw that the whole area had been turned over to agriculture and Cherent told me that some of the richest Ethiopian farmers came from the Asela area. I found this fact very depressing, the more so when, after Asela, we passed through a beautiful moorland reminiscent of the Simien Mountain moorland, that was probably going to completely disappear within the next couple of decades.

Third, although I had volunteered to do this trip I had previously avoided visiting the place for I was a Simien fan and disliked people telling me that Bale had more to offer. Also Bale seemed to attract more wildlife researchers than any other park. I find these people somewhat irritating because what they do seems rather self-seeking; apart from attracting some attention to a park their work is rarely of any direct benefit to nature conservation which either succeeds or fails regardless of what wildlife biologists discover about natural history. But for me the worst of their activities is that they take away the romance of wild places. Peering into the secret lives of animals just makes them less wild and mysterious and consequently less intriguing. Far better to leave them alone and concentrate instead on securing the protection of the land they need to survive in.

Anyhow, our trip was exclusively for picking up someone's household effects. We didn't venture into the park and we were lucky enough not to encounter any *ferenji* so by the time we got back to Addis I was still no wiser about the attractions of Bale Mountain National Park with its Senati Plateau and lush Harange Forest.

Eighteen months later I decided it was time to go and have a proper look at the Bale mountains. Besides, I was determined to visit Sheikh Hussein's tomb and the Sof Omar Caves that lie to the east of Bale.

During the week preceding our departure freak unseasonal rain fell all over the south and south-east of the country. Ethiopian television showed people and cattle being washed away in flooding rivers, and hectares of crops and even villages going under water. I tried to turn a deaf ear to the news because I really wanted to make the long overdue trip, and the night before we were due to leave I packed the car, making sure to put in a winch and extra food supplies. Some people we knew had actually visited this same area the previous week and we were going to meet up with them for supper to find out what was the real situation.

In fact they corroborated the news. They themselves had not been able to reach Sof Omar because the dry-weather road was not passable. Furthermore they had not even succeeded in driving as far as the Senati Plateau because the cloud was so low on the mountains that it was impossible to see the way. It was a very discouraging report, and we decided that it was certainly not worth trying. An alternative journey could have been to the national parks in the very south of the country, but news soon came in that these parks were completely cut off too. The bridge over the Kulfo River on the road into Arba Minch (the town where the religious war took place) had collapsed and no traffic could go either in or out of town. The Nechisar National Park headquarters in Arba Minch was completely flooded not only by the river but because there had also been a break in the town water supply pipe. The park electricity cables had also washed away. The Arba Minch Crocodile Ranch was under water because Lake Abaya had risen several metres. We heard that some sensible crocodiles had taken the opportunity to make off into the lake.

The road out of Arba Minch into the Konso area was also washed away so it was impossible to reach Jinka, the stepping-off point for visitors going to either Mago or Omo National Parks. The situation in the parks was even worse for the sizeable Mago bridge on the road connecting the two parks had washed away and the warden's house in Omo National Park was under water. The floodwater levels were everywhere far higher than any in living memory.

In the past I had made several trips to these three parks that are not easy to get to at the best of times. However, with enough time to spare one can have a real African adventure with an itinerary that takes you to Nechisar, Mago and Omo. Here one can see not only Ethiopia's last bastions of natural savannah habitats and some of the biggest herds left in Africa of tiang, lesser kudu and eland, but also one can mix with an extraordinary diversity of cultures that preserve traditional ways of life hardly changed from what they were centuries ago. Seven distinct groups of people border on Mago Park and five on Omo Park.

One of the best trips I had made to the southern parks was on a seven-ton truck that was carrying drums of aviation fuel to Nechisar and Mago for an aerial survey. I had never ridden in a truck before and I was curious to find out what the 800 kilometre journey would be like. The driver, Shifferaw, was a big, jovial man who knew how to handle his machine, which is not always the case with many of the Ethiopian drivers. The driving system in Ethiopia is the duck-and-weave method that many westerners are uneasy with at first, though it has its practitioners in countries like France and Italy. Most westerners are trained to drive essentially in straight lines, keeping position in traffic by adjusting speed rather than direction. With the duck-and-weave method a driver negotiates the traffic by dodging oncoming cars and weaving round those going the same way. This creates an endlessly intertwining pattern of vehicles reminiscent of flocks of sheep or goats being herded through narrow gaps where each individual tries to be the first through. In fact, herds of livestock mingle freely with the traffic and even in Addis it is not uncommon for a flock of sheep to draw up alongside you at a traffic light.

The most important part of a vehicle is the horn. A driver and his horn are one – it is an extension of his persona. When irritated by the slowness or ugliness or whatever of other cars a driver will use his horn to express his mood, much as many people will drum their fingers on the steering wheel, or shake their heads in exaggerated disbelief. Many drivers seem to use the horn as some sort of Buck Rogers ray-gun that in a more ideal world would satisfyingly vaporise the car in front. Drivers who find their horns unsuitable for all occasions often resort to the five-fingered salute. Being familiar only with the western, or two-fingered, salute I asked what was the significance of the impressive-looking five-fingered version. It is to remind the recipient, I was told, that any one of at least five men could have been his or her father.

In the truck the going was pretty slow at the best of times, and like truck drivers everywhere Shifferaw devised things to cope with the tedium. His main diversion was to sing and he entertained himself and us for hours by singing with a beautiful voice that was strong and easily heard over the noisy engine.

One of the reasons why the going was so slow was having constantly to slow down or stop for livestock on the road. The children whose task it is to spend their days herding their father's animals not surprisingly like to graze them on the road verges so they can divert some of *their* tedium by watching the traffic go by. Or better still, they encourage the animals out onto the road to make the traffic stop so they can get a good look at the funny people inside the tourist cars. Every time donkeys or cattle blocked Shifferaw's way he would interrupt his song to stick his head out of the window and yell in his best English, 'Stupid animals!' As the day wore on and the endless roadblocks of livestock became more annoying he would extend the same epithet to the many people who seemed to delight in forcing vehicles to slow down for them too. 'Stupid animal!' Shifferaw would bellow and whereas a donkey takes this unflinchingly people so addressed often come back with juicy curses of their own. All of which helps to break the monotony.

You get to learn a lot about how livestock are going to respond to a vehicle while travelling in Ethiopia. Once when Shifferaw had to pull up for a goat in the road – which is unusual because goats usually disperse well ahead of your car – he remarked that it must be a very special goat. 'How do you mean, special?' I asked.

'Well,' Shifferaw said, 'it seems his ancestors have paid up or he would run away.' I hadn't the foggiest notion what he was

103

talking about and asked him to explain. 'Well,' he said, 'a long, long time ago the ancestors of the cattle, donkeys, sheep, goats and dogs all hired a truck to take them to a certain place. At the end of their journey the time came to pay. The cattle and the donkeys paid up in full and went their way. The sheep and the goats, however, while the transporter was settling with the donkeys, ran off into the bush without paying. Finally the dogs, after paying the transporter, realised they'd been cheated and had paid too much. That is why today the sheep and the goats, who have guilty consciences, run off the road as a vehicle approaches. The donkeys and cattle who have clear consciences have nothing to fear and so simply stand about. Dogs on the other hand always chase after you shouting for their money back. So you see,' said Shifferaw, 'a goat that stands his ground must be a very special goat.'

Shifferaw was a man of many tales and another of my favourites was about a truck driver, a friend of his, who drove a tipper-truck. One day the man was coming back empty from the southern part of Ethiopia and because he had no load he decided to take on a few quintals of coffee. This was quite illegal as all coffee being taken into Addis had to be taxed. His friend figured that when he reached the customs checkpoint he would pay off the officials and then make himself a bit of money selling the coffee in Addis. But things went badly for him because the men at the customs checkpoint refused his pay-off and instead insisted that he go under escort to the police station in the nearby town. A customs official jumped into the cab beside the driver and they headed off. A little way up the road they passed through a small village where the driver had several friends. He had to slow down near this village because it was on a steep hill. As the truck crept along he surreptitiously operated the tip lever and the bags of coffee slid out onto the road without the guard noticing. On arrival at the police station the driver complained bitterly that he had been unfairly arrested and that he was not carrying contraband coffee. 'Search,' he said, 'you won't find anything. This official is just trying to cause trouble for me.' Well, of course, the police searched and found nothing. A few days later the driver went back to the village and picked up his sacks of coffee from the villagers who had taken them off the road and stored them, for a small fee, in their huts.

We took the road out of town that branches to the east at Mojo, one fork going north to Assab, the other fork going south through the Rift Valley. Lake Ziway is the first point of interest on the southern route and the small town of Ziway is often full of tourists who have come bird-watching on the lake. It is also possible to take a boat across to one of the lake islands where there is an ancient church.

My main interest in Ziway was a small eating house well off the main road that served the best Ethiopian food I have ever tasted. Fortunately, Shifferaw agreed with me and we stopped there for a meal of fish, baked whole on an open fire and served with a very hot sauce. The proprietor was a very masculine looking woman with a handshake that almost crushed your hand and a voice that shattered glass, most unusual for an Ethiopian woman. Nevertheless, she certainly knew how to produce a good meal which we demolished like hungry hyenas. Then with bellies full we set off again.

This was the time for Shifferaw to get stuck into the *chat*, for like many truck drivers chewing *chat* was an essential part of his day. For a while his singing grew much louder, but by the end of the chewing session he always became very silent and morose. At that point we had to stop for a beer which got him singing again.

He sang incessantly as we left our Ziway restaurant and continued on our journey passing by the Rift Valley lakes, Langano, Abiata and Shala. Lake Langano is a very popular weekend resort for local tourists, who go there to swim and drive their boats around. Lake Abiata is a large salty pan, whereas Lake Shala lies in a 266-metre deep crater and is dotted with small volcanic islands. People visit these lakes to look for waterbirds, that are slowly diminishing because of the heavy human settlement in the area. There is one point on the road when you can look back and see the three lakes at once. This is a spectacular view and I had long since decided that it was better to look at the lakes from that spot then to actually visit them which was always a disappointment.

The first night we stopped in Shashemene. This was a good indication of how slowly the truck travelled for Shashemene is only 250 kilometres from Addis, and when travelling by car we usually use it as a lunch stop.

Shashemene marks the point where the main south road to Awassa, and then Kenya, branches east to Bale and south-west to Jinka. It has a higgledy-piggledy layout and is far from clean, but it is a bustling place with plenty of eating houses, bars and nightclubs.

The next day the truck ground its way up to Sodo, perched above the Rift Valley escarpment in an area well known for its maize cultivation. The town itself lies at the base of a large mountain, with excellent views over to Lake Abaya 30 kilometres away down in the Rift Valley. From Sodo we motored back into the Rift Valley and on to Arba Minch where we took a couple of nights break at the Bekele Molle hotel.

This hotel has a commanding view of the Nechisar National Park lying between lakes Abaya and Chamo. Lake Abaya has a reddish brown tinge brought about by some mineral in its water. In contrast, Lake Chamo has clear icy-blue water. Looking over the escarpment from the hotel down into the park one can see the magnificent ground-water forest that is supported by the high water table associated with the escarpment's numerous fresh-water springs. This ground-water forest is the only one of its kind in East Africa.

The central long-grass plains of the park which from a distance look quite white are not visible from the hotel but they are what give the park its name *nech sar* (white grass). Nechisar National Park ranks in the experience of many visitors as one of the most beautiful places anywhere in the tropical savannahs and within its 514 square kilometres one can see a plenitude of different animal species, including greater kudu, zebra, lion, leopard, hippopotamus, crocodile, klipspringer and many more.

The klipspringer is a very interesting little antelope which lives on all kinds of rocks not only on hillsides and mountain massifs but also in semi-desert and dry wooded areas. The rocks have to be associated with some kind of bush as a place of refuge is important for the animal. Generally, this little animal with its long, splayed hooves which give it grip as it bounds around the rocky ridges, is very shy. However, on an earlier journey when I stopped for a night at the Dejen hotel I saw one at close quarters. This male klipspringer lived in the hotel bar and he had done so for a couple of years. He would spend his time rubbing his face on the bar stools, and picking up bits and pieces to eat. What was extraordinary about the animal though was that every now and then he would take a sudden dislike to one of the customers and charge across the room at high speed and start butting the unfortunate victim with all his might. Of course because he was only a small animal he didn't do anyone any damage, but people who didn't know him were terrified by his surprise attacks and frequently fled the bar without finishing their drink. Unfortunately the next time I visited the hotel the klipspringer was nowhere to be seen. I presumed that a customer had taken more than offence at the animal's boisterous behaviour, taken the animal and quietly made a Sunday roast out of him.

Once, on a trip to the central plains in Nechisar National Park in the middle of the day, I was lucky enough to see a leopard walking furtively along the road in front of the car. When he knew we were following him he slunk off into the bushes at the roadside. Most of the park animals are very wild, so this sighting was a real bonus.

Our stop in Arba Minch on this journey did not leave us time to go game spotting in the park, and having delivered several drums of fuel to the Arba Minch airfield and made some minor repairs to the truck we set off to Jinka two days later.

Jinka is about 200 kilometres from Arba Minch. For the most part the road is not bad but there are some very rough, stony sections and normally the drive takes about eight hours. The last 50 kilometres before arriving in Jinka takes you up a steep escarpment and knowing that this would be long and heavy work for the truck we decided to spend a night in Konso, 90 kilometres from Arba Minch, and go through to Jinka the next day. It was a good decision because on the steep hills the following day we were averaging about nine kilometres per hour and the total journey of 138 kilometres between Konso and Jinka took us about fifteen hours.

The Konso area is always fascinating for the Konso people are sophisticated farmers who have extensively terraced their land. Their area is not very fertile even though they have a good rainfall, and their land is just a series of steep hillsides. However, the industrious Konso have made the most of their lot and with thousands of little dry stone walls supporting their terraces they have succeeded in combating erosion and produce plenty of food. They are known by everyone in Ethiopia to be very hard workers and if a taxing physical job is on offer the Konso will take it on with alacrity. For instance, Konso professional well-diggers are famous all over the country. Konso town itself does not have much to offer and the hotels are not to be recommended. Our night in Konso was spent drifting from bar to bar in order to get ourselves suitably intoxicated to be able to get to sleep in our rather unpleasant rooms.

We set off next morning for Jinka. The road descends a steep escarpment into the Rift Valley and after crossing the Weyto river eventually climbs up again into the highlands around Jinka. Around lunchtime we came to a small village, Key Afer, where Shifferaw looked forward to a good lunch. There's a small hotel and restaurant there run by a pleasant old man and his family. We chose a table and the proprietor's daughter came to take our orders. But everything we asked for was answered monotonously by *yelem*, meaning there isn't any. I forget what we ate in the end but it wasn't what we wanted. Shifferaw has only a few words of English but they sufficed for him to observe sourly that 'This, Yelem Restaurant.' The name stuck and it's now widely known as the Yelem Restaurant in Key Afer.

We stopped in Jinka for only one night, dropping off several drums of fuel at the airfield. We weren't familiar with the aerial survey programme but we knew that we had to drop fuel in Arba Minch, Jinka, Murle and Mago National Park. Jinka is a scruffy but busy little town, the capital of South Omo Zone. On a market day one has the chance to see Mursi tribesmen who have come to town to sell honey collected from traditional hives in and around the park. Having sold their honey they then spend the money in Jinka's bars. Many tourists are astounded to come across a group of nude people sitting drinking in a public bar, for Mursi men traditionally scorn clothes. The administration requires them to don loin cloths when in town but these tend to get lost as the night wears on.

There are about 5000 of these people who live to the north and west of Mago National Park. The amassing of herds of cattle is the great ambition of the Mursi and indeed of all the lowland tribes of the south-east. Though the basis of their economy is cultivation, livestock preoccupies everyone and in common with pastoral people everywhere they are forever fighting their neighbours over matters of territory. The Mursi men in particular are quite fearsome looking as they stride along with at most a loin cloth and the ubiquitous Kalashnikov balanced on their shoulders.

On one occasion we were trying to take a photograph of Mursi warriors armed with their automatic weapons. The men wanted to pose standing to attention for the picture, whereas we wanted them to walk naturally so that there was some action in the shot. They were told to walk and ignore the camera. This posed a problem – how to walk yet maintain a good pose. They solved it by walking sideways so as to keep facing the camera. It took some considerable persuasion with action demonstrations to get them just to walk through the bush in a casual, relaxed way.

People who know the Mursi well say they are for the most part a friendly race and many tourists who have had car breakdowns in their area have been helped by them. Others have reported less kindly treatment.

The women's appearance is off-putting not to say grotesque to some people at first encounter because of the clay lip plates they wear. An unmarried woman's lower lip is pierced and then progressively stretched by inserting an ever larger object into the hole. When the aperture is large enough a clay disc, indented like a pulley wheel, is squeezed into it. As the lip stretches ever-larger discs are forced in until the lip, now a loop, is so long it can sometimes be pulled right over the owner's head. The size of the lip plate determines the bride price with a large one bringing in 50 head of cattle for the woman's father.

Lip plates are also practised by another, related tribe in the area, the Surma, who live on the border of Omo National Park. The Surma have an even more warlike reputation than the Mursi and are apt to treat anyone who passes through their land in a very cavalier fashion. Once a Frenchman spent a month among the Surma taking photographs of Surma daily life. Before he began his project he and the Surma agreed on a fee for the work and he rashly paid in advance. Things went well to begin with and he took hundreds of photographs. At the month's end as he slept his last night in the village a man crept into his tent and stole all the exposed film. The Surma laughed when he complained about the theft and refused to return his film and so he went back to Europe broke and empty-handed.

Although the Surma see themselves primarily as cattlemen many of them live by digging for alluvial gold near the Akobo river. Dima inhabitants who want to dig for gold in the same area have to strike a deal with the Surma or they are shot by the tribesmen within a few days of setting foot in the area. Like all the tribes in the area the Surma are heavily armed with modern automatic rifles and they don't hesitate to use them. If any of these people want to hunt in the park they do so for they are not afraid of the park game scouts, who, unfortunately are not well trained and are armed only with ancient rifles that are the laughing stock of the poachers.

From Jinka the road descends a precipitous escarpment into Mago National Park. This would have been the quickest route for us to take, but the escarpment is not well built and we decided that it wouldn't be wise to drive the loaded truck down the hill. Nevertheless, this is the way four-wheel drive vehicles take visitors down to the park that occupies the northern end of the Omo Trough, a small branch of the main Rift Valley.

The park has many attractions with beautiful riverine forest lining two of its major rivers, and this opens out on to plains of savannah bush and woodlands. Mago and Omo are the last protected areas in Ethiopia where the visitor can still see herds of elephant and buffalo. Mago's buffalo are estimated to number about 2000 animals and there is a small population of about 200 elephant resident in the park. Other animals in the area include wild dog, lion, leopard, gerenuk, greater kudu, lesser kudu, waterbuck, bushbuck and many others. The total number of mammal species is 80.

As well as the Mursi people, other tribes living in the area include the Hamer who cultivate the land south-east of the park. The Karo live just outside the park on the east bank of the Omo. They are related to the Hamer people. The Muguji live on the banks of the Omo where it joins the Mago River. They not only cultivate but fish and hunt as well. The Banna people farm the high ground to the east of Mago National Park and one can often see these people on the road that approaches Jinka from Arba Minch. It is no longer possible anywhere in Africa to spend a more informative and enjoyable couple of weeks as you can in the Mago and Omo National Park areas.

To reach Omo from Mago one has to drive west and cross the Omo River on the ferry. The Omo park is in one of the remotest corners of Ethiopia and if there has been heavy rain it is impossible to visit the place. The park encloses some 4068 square kilometres on the west bank of the Omo River. It has a variety of riverine forest, savannah woodland and wide, open grassy plains. It boasts large herds of eland of up to a thousand strong, and the plains also support the world's largest population of tiang. Other interesting animals include oryx, ostrich, giraffe, lions and cheetah.

Because we couldn't descend the Mago escarpment in the truck it meant we had to leave Jinka on the same road as we had arrived and travel back through the hills down onto the Weyto Plain, about half way to Konso.

In the Weyto area there is a road that goes to the south-west, first through irrigated cotton and fruit farms and then through bleak volcanic country stretching all the way to the Kenya border. This road passes through a small town called Turmi where it joins another road that takes one into the Mago National Park without having to descend any escarpments. This was the road we used.

The first day out of Jinka we only drove as far as Turmi because in the middle of the day we came across a broken-down car. The owners of the car told us that they had been stuck on the roadside for 24 hours. It was a stinking hot day and although they were all sitting under a shady tree, the travellers were very, very thirsty and greeted our drinking water drum with enthusiasm. They begged us to tow them to Turmi. Of course we were obliged to do this, because if we didn't help them they would probably die as not many cars used this road. The going was slow and we arrived in Turmi late in the afternoon, so we decided to stay the night.

The Turmi hotel was worse than the Konso hotel, with unswept rooms and used bed linen. In fact it was an unhappy night, for just as we settled down to have a drink at the bar we heard the most terrible yelping. Some dog was in dire pain. On listening more intently, the crying animal seemed to be quite near to us. We then discovered that the people living in the hotel compound had tied up their starving dog, which had stolen some food, and were beating it to death. There really is a complete lack of consideration for animals in this country. First, you get a dog. Second, you starve your dog. Third, you beat it to death. Fourth, you get another dog, and so on. Anyhow, fortunately on this occasion, after lengthy negotiations, we managed to have the animal freed.

Incidents like this are most upsetting and can completely ruin an evening. On one journey we made in Tigray to explore the rock-hewn churches we stayed in a very pleasant hotel in Howzen. The hotel was built around a well-watered courtyard with lush green grass that contrasted with the dry surrounding country. Three fat sheep were grazing in the courtyard when we went off for the day to clamber up the hillsides to peer into the little cave-like churches. When we got back to the hotel two fat sheep were grazing in the courtyard beside the empty skin of the third. The evening meal was sheep *tibs*. I couldn't eat a thing. It would have been quite another matter if the hotel owner had taken the skin away, but to see it lying there beside its two living companions completely turned me off.

The drive from Turmi to the park the next day turned out to be a nightmare as there had been a lot of rain and the flat land was a sea of mud. We had to dig the truck out of the mud three times and we were on our last legs by the time we reached the safari hunter's camp at Murle. The camp was deserted apart from the caretaker staff. We had hoped to be able to persuade them to hire us rooms for the night so that we could clean up and

112

have a good meal. However, they were not prepared to do this because we hadn't made a booking and after a heated discussion they turned us out of the premises.

We set our camp beds and mosquito nets up under a tree near the river. We were carrying plenty of food with us but I was much too tired to start cooking so Shifferaw and Cherent said they would make the evening meal, and a very good meal it was too. It didn't take any of us very long to go to sleep that evening.

Next morning we dumped the required fuel on the Murle airstrip and made our way along a dry sandy track to the Mago National Park headquarters where we met up with the aerial survey team. They had just returned from an aerial count of the Omo National Park plains animals and had seen large numbers of tiang and eland. At some times of the year it is possible to see a profusion of these animals watering at the Illibai Hot Spring, about an hour's drive from the park headquarters out on the Illibai plains and this is where they had found them. The water at the spring where it bubbles to the surface in a series of blow holes is almost boiling hot, but as it flows away it rapidly cools and this is where not only wild animals, but also Bumi cattle drink. (The Bumi people are great warriors living in and to the south of the park. They and the Surma are traditional enemies forever fighting for control of the grazing lands of the Omo Valley.) The cooler water of the spring also supports a small marsh with lots of aquatic creatures.

One day we made our way through the fringing marsh to look at the blow holes and were surprised to see a frog apparently swimming around inside one. 'Look, how can that frog survive in the hot spring water?' someone asked. 'Let's get it out and have a look at it.' It was duly fished out and proved to be a very dead frog whose apparent movements had been caused by the swirling water. 'Oh dear, one hop too far.' said one of the onlookers. Well may he have said that for in Ethiopia you often feel like a frog in a marsh surrounding a hot spring – it's all too easy to make that ill-judged hop. I thought of all my own hops to faraway destinations that had landed me in one disastrous fix after another. Of hopping to Jima to be arrested for supposedly smuggling gold; hopping to the Blue Nile Gorge to be shot at;

113

hopping all the way to Magdala just to have to hop all the way back again; hopping into Danakalia to get lost.

On the way back to Addis just before we reached Konso, Cherent and I were reminiscing about some of our trips and about how we had almost hopped too far on several occasions. 'Well,' he said, 'you know that it's your fault that we keep having problems.'

'What do you mean, my fault?'

'In Ethiopia,' he replied, 'we believe it is very bad luck to travel by road with a female stranger on board.'

'But we've seen hundreds of trucks and cars carrying females. Some of them must have been strangers. These vehicles can't all be having problems.'

He roared with laughter. 'No, but those girls know what to do. You see, if you are a lone female traveller in Ethiopia you must carry five stones in your pocket wherever you go and then there will be no problems.'

'OK then,' I said. 'Stop the truck, Shifferaw.' I climbed down and selected five lucky-looking stones from the dusty road and put them in my pocket.

'Right you men,' I said as I climbed back into my seat. 'Now you have a properly equipped woman on board. Let's go.'

It seemed almost inevitable that what happened next was that the truck wouldn't start. Shifferaw banged and swore underneath the bonnet for a while and finally announced that the fuel pump was broken.

Four days later as we drove into Addis in the late afternoon I surreptitiously slipped my hand into my jeans pocket, pulled the five stones out and dropped them through the window on to the asphalt road. I realised at that moment that I really rather preferred the excitement of hopping almost too far.